CHRISTMAS COTTAGE

Lynette Jensen

*Country-cottage style decorating,
entertaining, collecting, and quilting inspirations
for creating your dream Christmas*

LANDAUER BOOKS

Copyright© 2001 by Landauer Corporation

Projects Copyright© 2001 by Lynette Jensen

This book was designed, produced, and published by Landauer Books

A division of Landauer Corporation

12251 Maffitt Road, Cumming, Iowa 50061

President: Jeramy Lanigan Landauer

Vice President: Becky Johnston

Managing Editor: Marlene Hemberger Heuertz

Art Director: Laurel Albright

Creative Director: Lynette Jensen

Photography: Craig Anderson and Amy Cooper

Photostyling: Lynette Jensen and Margaret Sindelar

Technical Writer: Sue Bahr

Graphic Technician: Stewart Cott

Technical Illustrator: Lisa Kirchoff

We also wish to thank the support staff of the Thimbleberries® Design Studio:
Sherry Husske, Virginia Brodd, Renae Ashwill, Ardelle Paulson, Kathy Lobeck,
Carla Plowman, Julie Jergens, Pearl Baysinger, Tracy Schrantz, Leone Rusch, and Julie Borg.
Also, Suzanne Maki for decorative painting and Sue Graff for window treatments.

This book is printed on acid-free paper.

Printed in U.S.A. 10 9 8 7 6 5 4 3 2 1

Library of Congress Cataloging-in-Publication Data available upon request.

ISBN: 1-890621-25-0

CHRISTMAS *for family* 14

CHRISTMAS *by the fire* 44

CHRISTMAS *on the porch* 76

CHRISTMAS *stars & stripes* 94

CHRISTMAS *for kids* 50

CHRISTMAS *outdoors* 70

CHRISTMAS *for friends* 106

CHRISTMAS *hideaway* 116

FOREWORD

My husband, Neil and I have been married for 35 years and as each Christmas season approaches we find ourselves just as excited about sharing our blessings with friends and family as we did our first Christmas together.

Even though our nest is empty, we find the holidays the perfect time to fill it again, if only for a short time. Our daughter Kerry returns with her husband, Trevor, and our son Matt is accompanied by his soon-to-be bride, Cinnamon. With Neil's mother, and my parents living nearby, and an abundance of friends who come to visit, we always seem to find ourselves in a house overflowing with guests—and the more the merrier!

To accommodate all this abundance, last summer we had an opportunity to acquire a small brick cottage that serves as inspiration for my many decorating and entertaining ideas as well as a welcome retreat for our family, friends, and out-of-town guests.

This past holiday season we went all out, and with help from the Thimbleberries® staff, dressed up the cottage for Christmas. I thought you might enjoy a tour and be inspired to adapt many of the decorating, entertaining, collecting, and quilting ideas to your own home for creating your dream Christmas.

Lynette Jensen

CHRISTMAS COTTAGE

According to the architect's original blueprints, this small brick cottage nestled among the trees was designed in May of 1933 for Mr. and Mrs. O. H. Englund with custom features that have remained unchanged to this day. From the copper-roofed bay window overlooking the tuck-under single-car garage, to the gently curved sidewalk leading to the handsome front entry door with its ornately trimmed overhang, the feeling is of solid comfort that has withstood the test of time. And, when it's time to deliver the seven-foot tall Christmas tree, what better way to complement a 1930's cottage than with a cherry-red 1949 Ford pickup!

Lend an air of antiquity to any house—old or new—with a garland of greens to grace the front window. For the center swag and the garland, Lynette uses evergreens twined with grapevine, pine cones, and dried autumn joy blossoms from her garden.

A complementary wreath fills the space between window and door, and additional greens and pine cones cover the wrought-iron railing. For the landing, Lynette adds a vintage church birdhouse and an old painted metal bushel basket filled with greens, twigs, and pine cones. (Last autumn before the ground froze, Lynette filled the front flower bed beneath the window with a forest of tree tops.)

Once inside, first impressions are of the feeling that Christmas is in the air. The cottage was built with an old-fashioned vestibule with pegs for hanging up coats and jackets instead of a coat closet. Lynette filled the small space with red and green floral accents enhanced by the welcoming sight of candles all aglow.

INTRODUCTION

In a charming guest cottage that reflects the joys of Christmas inside and out, Lynette Jensen shares her family recipes and design ideas including luminaries, gift wraps, ornaments, quilts, fabric inspirations, and a wonderful stenciled floor inspired by Thimbleberries® quilt block motifs.

On the following pages, you'll see how easy it is to build on the traditions of the past to create your own holiday home and fill it with memories that will last a lifetime.

You'll also find dozens of festive decorating and entertaining ideas—including fresh new ways to use greens and naturals indoors and outdoors. Step-by-step how-tos, illustrations, and full-size patterns provide a hands-on guide for creating a Christmas to remember—in every room of your holiday house!

CHRISTMAS *for family*

Merry Christmas

Treat your family to a festive collage of red, white, and green. Lynette fills the cottage living room with greens, pine cones, dried blossoms from the garden, quilts, and antiques. Special accents are the red and cream winged back chairs flanking the fireplace, a red and green tea cart holding a tea pot and mugs with a reindeer stag design, and the flannel Homestead Quilt designed by Lynette for Thimbleberries®.

For an alternative to the traditional tree stand for this magnificent floor to ceiling Fraser Fir, Lynette substitutes a wine barrel half that has a scalloped top and is painted green. The tree is loaded with sparkling snowflakes, apple ornaments, postcard gift boxes, and silver-garlanded sheet music cones.

BOXES THAT GO FROM PLAIN TO PERFECT. The perfect gift often begins with the perfect box. Each brown cardboard box in the trio shown above takes on true holiday spirit when festively wrapped.

ORNAMENTS THAT GO FROM TREE TO TABLE. Adding sparkle to any place setting, the sheet music cone ornament, top left, is simply a cone made from sheet music fused to wrapping paper, trimmed with antique silver garland and filled with German statice and berry sprigs.

GIFTS THAT GO FROM ORNAMENTS TO FAVORS. The box tree ornaments shown at left are made with vintage postcards, cover stock, and ribbons. A change in ribbon width makes the transformation into small gift boxes for party favors.

The Sheet Music Cone is shown on page 17 and measures 7-inches long.

WHAT YOU'LL NEED

**2, 7 x 8-inch pieces of
Assorted WRAPPING PAPER
or SHEET MUSIC
for outside and inside of cone**

**7 x 8-inch piece of
ultra hold HEAT 'N BOND®**

**1/3 yard of 1-inch wide
RIBBON for tie**

Optional:
**24-inch length of Antique
Silver Garland for trim**

**12-inch length of
Pearl Cotton or
1/8-inch wide Ribbon for hanger**

**3/4-inch diameter Decorative Button
for hanger attachment**

Glue

Paper punch with 1/8-inch hole

Cone Assembly

Step 1 Following the Heat 'N Bond® instructions, adhere the 2 pieces of wrapping paper or sheet music together.

Step 2 Make a cone template using the pattern on page 19. Lay the cone template on the fused wrapping paper. Trace around the cone template and cut on the line. Punch out the holes where indicated.

Step 3 Overlap the cone edges where indicated on the pattern. Thread the 1-inch wide ribbon through the holes and tie.

Optional

Step 1 If adding antique silver garland, carefully glue it in place along edge of cone.

Step 2 If using the cone as an ornament, glue or sew a button to the inside of the cone at the center back. Tie pearl cotton or the 1/8-inch wide ribbon around the button to use as a hanger.

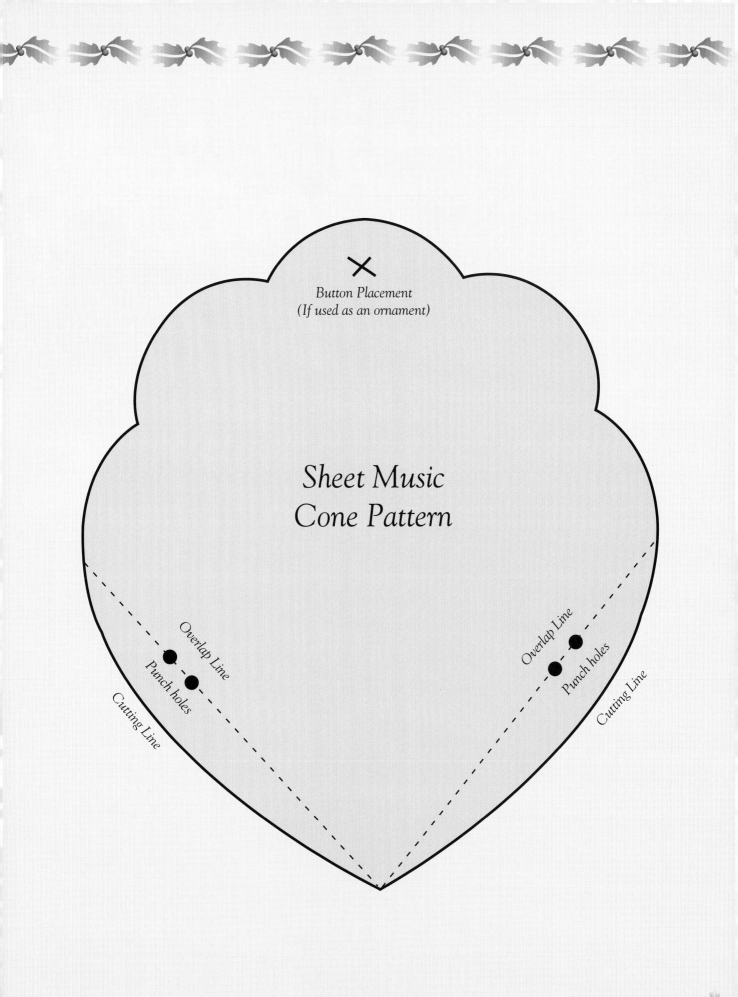

The Box Tree Ornament is shown on page 17 and measures 3-1/4 x 6-inches.

WHAT YOU'LL NEED

8-1/2 x 11-inch sheet of
CARD STOCK per ornament

1-1/2 yards of 1/4-inch
wide GOLD RIBBON

GLUE

X-ACTO® KNIFE

ANTIQUE POSTCARDS

Box Tree Ornament

Step 1 Trace box shape onto the 8-1/2 x 11-inch card stock paper. Cut into box shape.

Step 2 Using an X-Acto® knife, score the curved lines on the outside of the box, taking care not to cut all the way through the paper.

Step 3 Fold along the fold lines.

Step 4 Place glue along the side-flap. Turn the flap to the inside of the box and hold until glue sets.

Step 5 Fold in the end flaps.

Step 6 Glue postcards to the box front. Optional: postcards may be trimmed with a decorative edging scissors.

Step 7 Tie a ribbon around the box over both sides of the postcard. Tie a third piece of ribbon to each of the first two ribbons to form a hanger at the top of the box. If making a gift box, tie a wider ribbon to one side of the postcard and fill with small treasures and treats.

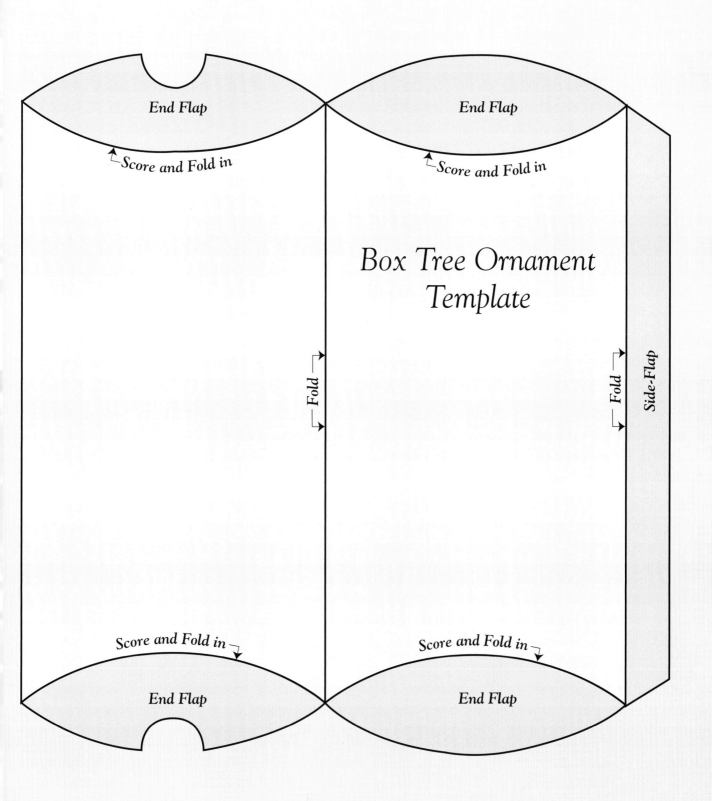

End Flap

Score and Fold in

End Flap

Score and Fold in

Box Tree Ornament
Template

Fold

Fold

Side-Flap

Score and Fold in

Score and Fold in

End Flap

End Flap

Christmas for family

Symbols of the season—reindeer and pine trees—
are paired in this inviting holiday setting.
The reindeer stag tea service is from Lynette's
extensive collection, and the Patchwork Pines
Quilt is one of many she has designed for
Thimbleberries®. Underfoot, the well-worn hooked
rug dating from the 1930's is a keepsake with badly
frayed edges. They were easily repaired by adding
a wide binding of black and cream checked fabric.

AN OLD RUG'S NEW COUNTERPART.
An antique pine trunk, right, showcases
a tulip-filled pewter pitcher and a newly-
hooked table rug inspired by the 1930's
floor rug.

PINE TREES THAT NEVER NEED
WATERING. Pine trees will be perpetual
evergreens when pieced in patchwork.
Lynette's Patchwork Pines Quilt is the
perfect complement to any red, white,
and green decorating scheme.

The Patchwork Pines Quilt is shown
on page 22 and measures 46-inches square.

WHAT YOU'LL NEED

Yardage is based on 42-inch wide fabric

7/8 yard GREEN PRINT for trees,
inner border, and pieced border

1 yard BEIGE PRINT for
background and
checkerboard border

1/2 yard RED PRINT #1
for lattice and pieced border

1/4 yard GOLD PRINT
for star and corner squares

1/4 yard BLACK PRINT
for checkerboard border

7/8 yard RED PRINT #2
for outer border

1/2 yard BLACK PRINT
for binding

2-3/4 yards Backing fabric

Quilt batting, at least
50-inches square

Tree Blocks (Make 4)

Cutting

From GREEN PRINT:
- Cut 2, 2-7/8 x 42-inch strips
- Cut 4, 4-1/2-inch squares
- Cut 4, 2-1/2-inch squares
- Cut 4, 1-3/4 x 9-inch rectangles

From BEIGE PRINT:
- Cut 2, 2-7/8 x 42-inch strips
- Cut 6, 1-1/2 x 42-inch strips.
  From these strips cut:

8, 1-1/2 x 12-1/2-inch rectangles
8, 1-1/2 x 10-1/2-inch rectangles
- Cut 4, 6-1/2-inch squares
- Cut 8, 2-1/2-inch squares

Piecing

Step 1   With right sides together, layer the
2-7/8 x 42-inch GREEN and BEIGE
strips in pairs. Press together, but do not
sew. Cut the layered strips into squares.
Cut the layered squares in half diagonally
to make 56 sets of triangles. Stitch
1/4-inch from the diagonal edge of each
pair of triangles, and press. At this point
each triangle-pieced square should measure
2-1/2-inches square.

Crosscut 28, 2-7/8-inch squares   *Make 56, 2-1/2-inch
triangle-pieced squares*

Step 2   Draw a diagonal line on each of the
6-1/2-inch BEIGE squares, but do not cut.

Step 3 Fold the 1-3/4 x 9-inch GREEN rectangles in half lengthwise, wrong sides together, and press. Position the GREEN rectangle on the BEIGE square so that the raw edges are even with the diagonal line. Stitch together with a 1/4-inch seam allowance. Fold the GREEN rectangle over the raw edges and hand-stitch in place.

Make 4

Step 4 Referring to the diagram, position a 4-1/2-inch GREEN square on the upper corner of the Step 3 unit. Draw a diagonal line on the GREEN square, and stitch on the line. Trim the seam allowances to 1/4-inch, and press. Repeat at the opposite corner of the BEIGE square with a 2-1/2-inch GREEN square, as shown.

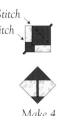

Stitch
Stitch

Make 4

Step 5 Sew together 3 of the Step 1 triangle-pieced squares, and press. Sew the units together in pairs, and press. Sew the units to the top of the Step 4 units, and press. At this point each unit should measure 6-1/2 x 10-1/2-inches.

Make 8   *Make 4*   *Make 4*

Step 6 Sew together 3 of the Step 1 triangle-pieced squares, and press. Sew the units together in pairs, and press. At this point each unit should measure 4-1/2 x 6-1/2-inches.

Make 8   *Make 4*

Step 7 Sew the remaining Step 1 triangle-pieced squares and the 2-1/2-inch BEIGE squares together in pairs, and press. Sew these pairs together, and press. At this point each unit should measure 4-1/2-inches.

Make 8

Make 4

Step 8 Sew the Step 7 units to the top of the Step 6 units, and press. Sew the units to the right edge of the Step 5 units, and press. At this point each tree block should measure 10-1/2-inches square.

Make 4

Step 9 Sew the 1-1/2 x 10-1/2-inch BEIGE strips to the top and bottom of the tree blocks, and press. Sew the 1-1/2 x 12-1/2-inch BEIGE strips to the sides of the tree blocks to complete the block, and press. At this point each block should measure 12-1/2-inches square.

Make 4

Quilt Center

Cutting

From RED PRINT #1:
- Cut 2, 4-1/2 x 42-inch strips. From these strips cut: 4, 4-1/2 x 12-1/2-inch rectangles

From GOLD PRINT:
- Cut 1, 4-1/2-inch center square
- Cut 1, 2-1/2 x 42-inch strip. From this strip cut: 16, 2-1/2-inch squares. Set 8 squares aside for corner squares.

Piecing

Step 1 Position a 2-1/2-inch GOLD square on the corner of a 4-1/2 x 12-1/2-inch RED rectangle. Draw a diagonal line on the GOLD square and stitch on the line.

Trim the seam allowance to 1/4-inch, and press. Repeat this process on the adjacent corner of the RED rectangle, and press.

Make 4

Step 2 Referring to the quilt diagram for placement, sew a tree block to both sides of a Step 1 lattice strip. Press the seam allowances toward the tree blocks. Make 2 block rows.

Step 3 Sew the remaining Step 1 lattice strips to both sides of the 4-1/2-inch GOLD square. Press the seam allowances toward the GOLD square.

Step 4 Referring to the quilt diagram for placement, sew the block rows to both sides of the Step 3 lattice strip, and press.

Borders

Note: *The yardage given allows for the border strips to be cut on the crosswise grain. Diagonally piece the strips as needed, referring to page 139 for Diagonal Piecing Instructions.*

Cutting
From GREEN PRINT:
- Cut 8, 1-1/2 x 42-inch inner border and pieced border strips

From RED PRINT #1:
- Cut 4, 1-1/2 x 42-inch pieced border strips

From BLACK PRINT:
- Cut 2, 2-1/2 x 42-inch strips for the checkerboard border

From BEIGE PRINT:
- Cut 2, 2-1/2 x 42-inch strips for the checkerboard border

From RED PRINT #2:
- Cut 5, 4-1/2 x 42-inch outer border strips

From GOLD PRINT:
- Use the 8, 2-1/2-inch corner squares cut earlier

Assembling and Attaching the Borders

Step 1 To attach the 1-1/2-inch wide GREEN inner border strips, refer to page 138 for Border Instructions.

Step 2 To make the checkerboard border, aligning long edges, sew the 2-1/2 x 42-inch BLACK and BEIGE strips together in pairs. Refer to page 138 for Hints and Helps for Pressing Strip Sets. Cut the strip sets into segments.

Crosscut 32, 2-1/2-inch wide segments

Step 3 For each checkerboard border, sew 8 of the Step 2 segments together. Make 4 checkerboard border strips. Remove a 2-1/2-inch BEIGE square from each checkerboard border. At this point each border strip should measure 2-1/2 x 30-1/2-inches. Sew border strips to the top and bottom edges of the quilt center, and press.

Step 4 Add 2-1/2-inch GOLD corner squares to both ends of the remaining checkerboard border strips, and press. Sew the border strips to the sides of the quilt center, and press.

Make 2

Step 5 Aligning long edges, sew together the 1-1/2 x 42-inch RED PRINT #1 strips and the remaining 1-1/2 x 42-inch GREEN strips in pairs, and press. Measure the quilt center from left to right through the center to determine the length of the pieced border strips. Cut 4 RED/GREEN pieced border strips to this length. Sew pieced border strips to the top and bottom of the quilt center, and press.

Step 6 Add 2-1/2-inch GOLD corner squares to both ends of the remaining pieced border strips, and press. Sew the border strips to the sides of the quilt center, and press.

Step 7 To attach the 4-1/2-inch wide RED PRINT #2 outer border strips, refer to page 138 for Border Instructions.

Putting It All Together

Cut the 2-3/4 yard length of backing fabric in half crosswise to make 2, 1-3/8 yard lengths. Refer to Finishing the Quilt on page 139 for complete instructions.

Binding

Cutting

From BLACK PRINT:
- Cut 5, 2-3/4 x 42-inch strips

Sew the binding to the quilt using a 3/8-inch seam allowance. This measurement will produce a 1/2-inch wide finished double binding. Refer to page 139 for Binding and Diagonal Piecing Instructions.

Patchwork Pines Quilt

Christmas for family

Lynette carries color around the room to brighten dark corners and furniture, and adds a touch of white whenever possible. Opposite, an unusual pine jelly cupboard with screens in the doors, is home to a colorful collection of red and green quilts.

ADD A MANTEL OF WHITE. Just as new fallen snow whitens everything outdoors, a dusting of white will do the same indoors as shown on the impressive flocked wreath shown at right. The mantel is host to a swag of pine cones interspersed with red beads, and topped with an artificial white berry garland, greenery, dried hydrangeas, and sugar pine cones.

MAY ALL YOUR CHRISTMASES BE WHITE. For the holidays, set the books aside and fill the shelves with white porcelain. The vases showcased, right, are mostly Shawnee and McCoy from Lynette's collection. For greater impact, each white vase is surrounded by a soft carpet of greens and displayed individually.

 Homestead Quilt

The Homestead Quilt is shown on page 15 and measures 58 x 70-inches.

WHAT YOU'LL NEED

Yardage is based on 42-inch wide fabric

1 yard GREEN SOLID
for doors, roofs, and middle border

7/8 yard RED PRINT
for houses and corner squares

1-1/2 yards GREEN PLAID
for houses and outer border

1/2 yard BROWN PRINT
for houses

1/4 yard GOLD SOLID
for windows

2 yards BEIGE PRINT for background for houses and flying geese, and lattice and inner border

1/3 yard each of 4 Coordinating DARK FABRICS for flying geese units (Brown Plaid, Green Solid, Brown Print, Chestnut Solid)

2/3 yard GREEN SOLID
for binding

3-1/2 yards Backing fabric

Quilt batting, at least
62 x 74-inches

House Blocks (Make 12)

Cutting

From GREEN SOLID:
- Cut 2, 2-1/2 x 42-inch strips.
  From these strips cut:
  12, 2-1/2 x 4-1/2-inch rectangles
- Cut 3, 3-1/2 x 42-inch strips.
  From these strips cut:
  12, 3-1/2 x 4-1/2-inch rectangles
  12, 3-1/2-inch squares

From RED PRINT:
- Cut 4, 1-1/2 x 42-inch strips.
  From these strips cut:
  24, 1-1/2 x 4-1/2-inch rectangles
  24, 1-1/2-inch squares
- Cut 4, 3-1/2 x 42-inch strips.
  From these strips cut:
  12, 3-1/2 x 6-1/2-inch rectangles
  12, 3-1/2 x 4-1/2-inch rectangles

From GREEN PLAID:
- Cut 5, 1-1/2 x 42-inch strips.
  From these strips cut:
  24, 1-1/2 x 7-1/2-inch rectangles
- Cut 2, 2-1/2 x 42-inch strips.
  From these strips cut:
  24, 2-1/2-inch squares

From BROWN PRINT:
- Cut 7, 1-1/2 x 42-inch strips.
  From these strips cut:
  24, 1-1/2 x 7-1/2-inch rectangles
  24, 1-1/2 x 2-1/2-inch rectangles
- Cut 1, 2-1/2 x 42-inch strip.
  From this strip cut:
  12, 2-1/2-inch squares

From GOLD SOLID:
- Cut 1, 1-1/2 x 42-inch strip.
  From this strip cut:
  12, 1-1/2 x 2-1/2-inch rectangles
- Cut 1, 2-1/2 x 42-inch strip.
  From this strip cut:
  12, 2-1/2-inch squares

From BEIGE PRINT:
- Cut 2, 3-1/2 x 42-inch strips.
  From these strips cut:
  24, 3-1/2-inch squares

Piecing

Step 1 Sew 1-1/2 x 4-1/2-inch RED rectangles to both sides of a 2-1/2 x 4-1/2-inch GREEN SOLID rectangle, and press.

Make 12

Step 2 Position a 2-1/2-inch GREEN PLAID square on the corner of a 3-1/2 x 4-1/2-inch RED rectangle. Draw a diagonal line on the GREEN square, and stitch on this line. Trim the seam allowance to 1/4-inch, and press. Repeat this process on the adjacent corner of the RED rectangle. Sew this unit to the top of the Step 1 unit, and press.

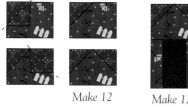

Make 12   Make 12

Step 3 Position a 1-1/2-inch RED square on the corner of a 1-1/2 x 7-1/2-inch GREEN PLAID rectangle. Referring to the diagrams, draw a diagonal line on the RED square, and stitch on the line. Trim the seam allowance to 1/4-inch and press. Sew the units to both sides of the Step 2 unit, and press.

Make 12   Make 12   Make 12

Step 4 Position a 3-1/2-inch GREEN SOLID square on the left-hand corner of a 3-1/2 x 6-1/2-inch RED rectangle. Draw a diagonal line on the GREEN SOLID square, and stitch on this line. Trim the seam allowance to 1/4-inch, and press. Repeat this process at the opposite corner of the RED rectangle using a 3-1/2-inch BEIGE square. Sew this unit to the top of the Step 3 unit, and press. At this point each unit should measure 6-1/2 x 10-1/2-inches.

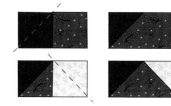

Make 12

Make 12

Step 5 Sew together 2, 1-1/2 x 2-1/2-inch BROWN rectangles, a 1-1/2 x 2-1/2-inch GOLD rectangle, a 2-1/2-inch GOLD square, and a 2-1/2-inch BROWN square, and press. Sew a 1-1/2 x 7-1/2-inch BROWN rectangle to both sides of this unit, and press.

Make 12

Step 6 Position a 3-1/2-inch BEIGE square on the left-hand corner of a 3-1/2 x 4-1/2-inch GREEN SOLID rectangle. Draw a diagonal line on the BEIGE square and stitch on this line. Trim the seam allowance to 1/4-inch, and press. Sew this unit to the top of the Step 5 unit, and press.

Make 12

Step 7 Sew the Step 4 unit to the right-hand side of this unit, and press. At this point each house block should measure 10-1/2-inches square.

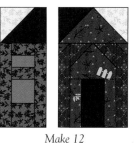

Make 12

Quilt Center

Note: *The yardage given allows for the lattice and border strips to be cut on the crosswise grain. Diagonally piece the strips as needed, referring to page 139 for Diagonal Piecing Instructions.*

Cutting

From BEIGE PRINT:
- Cut 10, 2-1/2 x 42-inch strips.
  From these strips cut:
  2, 2-1/2 x 50-1/2-inch side inner border strips
  2, 2-1/2 x 46-1/2-inch lattice strips
  2, 2-1/2 x 34-1/2-inch top
    and bottom inner border strips
  9, 2-1/2 x 10-1/2-inch lattice strips

Piecing

Step 1 Referring to the quilt diagram, sew together a vertical row of 4 house blocks and 3, 2-1/2 x 10-1/2-inch BEIGE lattice strips, and press. Make 3 of these vertical block rows.

Step 2 Referring to the quilt diagram, sew together the 3 block rows and the 2, 2-1/2 x 46-1/2-inch BEIGE lattice strips, and press.

Step 3 Sew the 2-1/2 x 34-1/2-inch BEIGE top and bottom inner border strips to the quilt center, and press.

Step 4 Sew the 2-1/2 x 50-1/2-inch BEIGE side border strips to the quilt center, and press. At this point the quilt center should measure 38-1/2 x 50-1/2-inches.

Borders

Note: *The yardage given allows for the border strips to be cut on the crosswise grain. Diagonally piece the strips as needed, referring to page 139 for Diagonal Piecing Instructions.*

Cutting

From GREEN SOLID:
- Cut 5, 2-1/2 x 42-inch middle border strips

From *each* of the 4 Coordinating DARK FABRICS:
- Cut 3, 2-1/2 x 42-inch strips.
  From these strips cut:
  24, 2-1/2 x 4-1/2-inch rectangles for a *total* of 96, 2-1/2 x 4-1/2-inch rectangles

From BEIGE PRINT:
- Cut 12, 2-1/2 x 42-inch strips.
  From these strips cut:
  192, 2-1/2-inch squares for the flying geese background

From RED PRINT:
- Cut 1, 4-1/2 x 42-inch strip.
  From this strip cut:
  4, 4-1/2-inch corner squares

From GREEN PLAID:
- Cut 7, 4-1/2 x 42-inch outer border strips

Piecing and Attaching the Borders

Step 1 To attach the 2-1/2-inch wide GREEN SOLID middle border strips, refer to page 138 for Border Instructions.

Step 2 To make the flying geese units, position a 2-1/2-inch BEIGE square on the corner of each 2-1/2 x 4-1/2-inch DARK rectangle. Draw a diagonal line on the BEIGE squares, and stitch on the line. Trim the seam allowances to 1/4-inch, and press. Repeat this process at the opposite corner of each DARK rectangle. At this point each unit should measure 2-1/2 x 4-1/2-inches.

Make a total of 96 flying geese units

Step 3 To make the top and bottom pieced borders, sew 21 flying geese units together in a random fashion, and press. Refer to the quilt diagram for orientation of the flying geese units. Sew the border strips to the top and bottom of the quilt, and press.

Make 2

Step 4 To make the side pieced borders, sew 27 flying geese units together in a random fashion, and press. Sew 4-1/2-inch RED corner squares to the ends of these strips, and press. Refer to the quilt diagram for orientation of the flying geese units. Sew the border strips to the sides of the quilt, and press.

Make 2

Step 5 To attach the 4-1/2-inch wide GREEN PLAID outer border strips, refer to page 138 for Border Instructions.

Putting It All Together

Cut the 3-1/2 yard length of backing fabric in half crosswise to make 2, 1-3/4 yard lengths. Refer to Finishing the Quilt on page 139 for complete instructions.

Binding

Cutting

From GREEN SOLID:
• Cut 7, 3 x 42-inch strips

Sew the binding to the quilt using a 3/8-inch seam allowance. This measurement will produce a 1/2-inch wide finished double binding. Refer to page 139 for Binding and Diagonal Piecing Instructions.

Homestead Quilt

The Festive Bow Ties Wall Quilt is shown on page 29 and measures 9-1/2-inches square.

WHAT YOU'LL NEED

Yardage is based on 42-inch wide fabric

4-inch square each of **9 ASSORTED DARK PRINTS** for bows

4-inch square each of **9 ASSORTED TAN PRINTS** for background

1/8 yard BLACK PRINT for inner border and binding

1/8 yard GOLD PRINT for outer border

12-inch square Backing Fabric

Quilt Batting, at least **12-inches square**

Bow Tie Blocks (Make 9)

Cutting

From *each* ASSORTED DARK PRINT:
- Cut 2, 1-1/2-inch squares
- Cut 2, 1-inch squares

From *each* ASSORTED TAN PRINT:
- Cut 2, 1-1/2-inch squares

Piecing

Step 1   Position a 1-inch DARK square on the corner of a 1-1/2-inch TAN square. Draw a diagonal line on the DARK square and stitch on the line. Trim the seam allowance to 1/4-inch and press. Repeat this process using the same DARK and TAN fabrics so that you will have two identical units for each block.

  Make 2 units using each DARK PRINT/TAN PRINT combination

Step 2   Sew each of the Step 1 units to a corresponding 1-1/2-inch DARK square and press. Sew the corresponding units together in pairs and press. At this point each bow tie block should measure 2-1/2-inches square.

Make 2

Make a bow tie block using each DARK PRINT/ TAN PRINT combination

Step 3   Referring to the quilt diagram, sew the blocks together in 3 rows of 3 blocks each. Press the seam allowances in alternating directions by rows so the seams will fit snugly together with less bulk.

Step 4   Pin the rows at the block intersections and sew the rows together. Press the seam allowances in one direction.

Borders

Note: The yardage given allows for the border strips to be cut on the crosswise grain.

Cutting

From BLACK PRINT:
- Cut 1, 1 x 42-inch inner border strip

From GOLD PRINT:
- Cut 1, 1-1/2 x 42-inch outer border strip

Attaching the Borders

Step 1   To attach the 1-inch wide BLACK inner border strips, refer to page 138 for Border Instructions.

Step 2   To attach the 1-1/2-inch wide GOLD outer border strips, refer to page 138 for Border Instructions.

Putting It All Together

Trim the backing fabric and batting so they are 2-inches larger than the quilt top. Refer to Finishing the Quilt on page 139 for complete instructions.

Binding

Cutting

From BLACK PRINT:
- Cut 1, 2-1/4 x 42-inch strip

Sew the binding to the quilt using a 1/4-inch seam allowance. This measurement will produce a 1/4-inch wide finished double binding. Refer to page 139 for Binding and Diagonal Piecing Instructions.

Festive Bow Ties Wall Quilt

Autumn accents of dried naturals and fresh greens fill large open areas and small corners with color and texture. Use them liberally for almost effortless decorating drama.

EXPERIENCE THE EVERLASTING EFFECTS OF AUTUMN'S HARVEST. In late summer Lynette begins preserving large blossoms from the hydrangea bushes that bloom in abundance in her garden. At Christmastime, as shown above, she combines them with other dried florals and greens in a vintage wicker backpack to create a stunning winter bouquet, or clusters them in a graceful garland for the staircase shown below left.

EMPHASIZE TRADITIONAL COLORS. For splashes of red and green color, Lynette displays beautifully wrapped packages and, on the tabletop above, a red-roofed needlepoint cottage doorstop. Ironstone pitchers and fresh flowers add a dash of winter white to the mix. Additional color comes from her book-shelf display of antique plates featuring wildlife and holly motifs accented with greens and green China berries.

Christmas for family

Discovering new and unusual ways to add interest to the walls is one of Lynette's favorite challenges. This framed collection of handmade wool ornaments showcases the stitching detail of each ornament. The leaf wall stencil, below, provides subtle color and dimension.

It takes a village. Lynette designed the wool and buttonhole-stitched Country Village Ornaments, above, to be used on a tree or framed for use on the wall as shown above.

Replicate striped wallpaper with stencils and paint. At right, leaf-shaped stencils add soft color and feather-like ambience to the walls. Lynette finds that stencils and paint are easier to apply to walls and far less costly than wallpaper. The leaf stencil was used in an overall random pattern on the adjoining dining room walls.

The Country Village Ornaments shown here measure from 3-1/2-inches to 4-1/2-inches tall.

WHAT YOU'LL NEED

Template material

The fabric amounts given in instructions below are for one ornament each.

Country Village Ornaments

Church:

- 1, 5 x 6-inch rectangle WHITE WOOL for church and steeple
- 2, 5 x 6-inch rectangles GREEN WOOL for background behind church
- 2, 5 x 6-inch rectangles FUSIBLE WEB
- Cotton print FABRIC SCRAPS and FUSIBLE WEB for window, door, etc.
- Gold, black, and red Embroidery Floss or #8 Pearl Cotton

House or Store:

- 1, 4-1/2-inch square COLORED WOOL for building
- 2, 5-inch squares BLACK WOOL for background behind building
- 1, 4-1/2-inch square FUSIBLE WEB
- 1, 5-inch square FUSIBLE WEB
- Cotton print FABRIC SCRAPS and FUSIBLE WEB for windows, doors, chimneys, etc.
- Red and black Embroidery Floss or #8 Pearl Cotton

Tree:

- 1, 4-1/2-inch square GREEN WOOL for tree
- 2, 5-inch squares BLACK WOOL for background behind tree

- 1, 4-1/2-inch square FUSIBLE WEB
- 1, 5-inch square FUSIBLE WEB
- Light gold, red, and variegated Embroidery Floss or #8 Pearl Cotton

Star:

- 1, 4-1/2-inch square BROWN WOOL for star
- 2, 5-inch squares BLACK WOOL for background behind star
- 1, 4-1/2-inch square FUSIBLE WEB
- 1, 5-inch square FUSIBLE WEB
- Light gold and red Embroidery Floss or #8 Pearl Cotton

General Instructions for Church, House, and Store

All houses, stores and church use three basic shapes. By adding chimneys, windows, doors and other details, you can change each building.

Step 1 Trace the building and details onto template material or paper.

Step 2 Apply fusible web to one side of the colored wool fabric for the building.

Step 3 Place the building template on the paper side of the wool 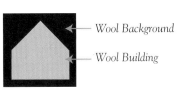 square and trace. Cut out the shape, and remove the paper backing.

Wool Background

Wool Building

Step 4 Fuse the wool building to 1 piece of wool backing (green for the church and black for the other buildings).

Step 5 Apply fusible web to the wrong side of the fabric scraps for building details. Place the paper detail patterns on the paper side of the fabric scraps and trace around the outer edges. Cut out detail shapes and remove paper backing.

Step 6 Position and fuse the details to the building.

Step 7 Using 3 strands of black embroidery floss (or pearl cotton), buttonhole stitch over the edges of the details into the building fabric and over the outer edges of building into background fabric.

Step 8 Apply fusible web to one side of the remaining piece of background fabric. Remove the backing paper and fuse to the wrong side of the assembled building to cover the back side of the stitches and add body to the completed ornament.

Cut 1/4-inch from outer edge of building

Step 9 Cut out the building shape, cutting 1/4-inch from the outer edges of the building (and chimney or steeple if being used).

Step 10 With 3 strands of red embroidery floss (or pearl cotton) buttonhole stitch over the raw edges of the background.

Step 11 To hang the ornament, add a loop of embroidery floss or pearl cotton at the top.

General Instructions for Trees and Stars

Step 1 Trace the tree and star pattern pieces onto template material or paper.

Step 2 Apply fusible web to the one side of the GREEN wool square for the tree or to the BROWN wool square for the star.

Step 3 Place tree or star template on the paper side of the wool square. Trace, cut out the shape, and remove the paper backing.

Step 4 Fuse the wool tree or star shape to a black wool square.

Step 5 With 3 strands of light gold embroidery floss (or pearl cotton), buttonhole stitch over the outer edges of the star or tree through the background fabric as shown for the buildings.

Step 6 With 3 strands of variegated embroidery floss, make French knots on the tree for lights; use an outline stitch for star details.

Step 7 Apply fusible web to one side of the remaining black background square. Remove the backing paper and fuse to the wrong side of the ornament.

Step 8 Cut out the star or tree shape, cutting 1/4-inch from the outer edges.

Step 9 With 3 strands of red embroidery floss (or pearl cotton), buttonhole stitch over the edges of the black background shape. Add a hanging loop as shown for the buildings.

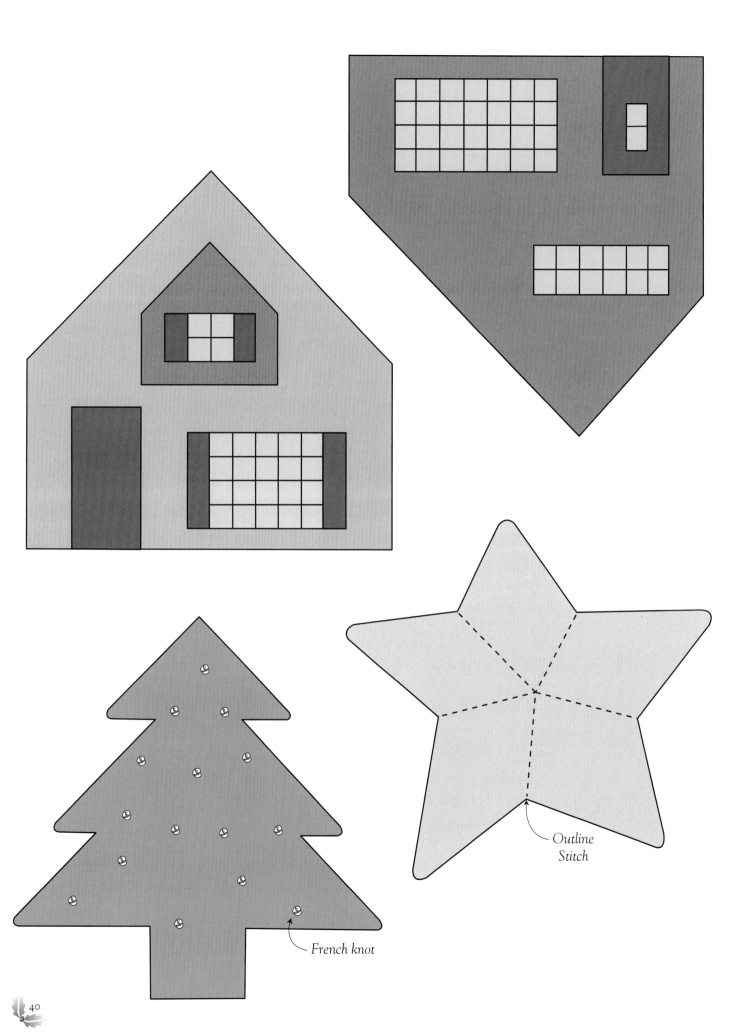

French knot

Outline
Stitch

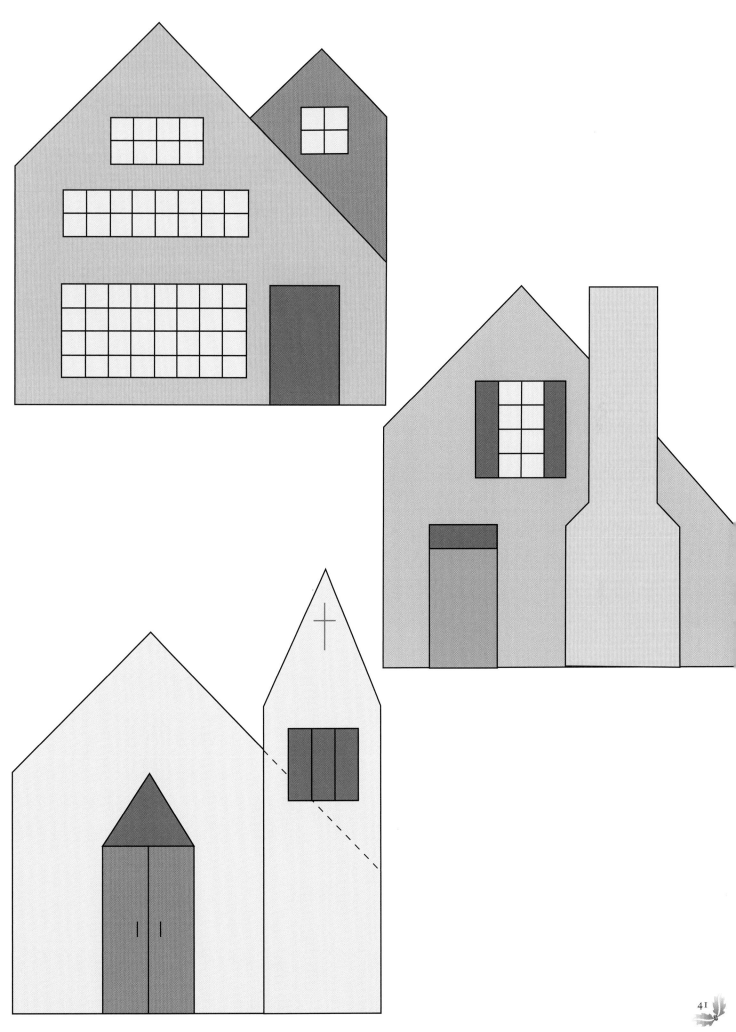

Leaf Stenciling

The leaf stenciling is shown on page 37.

WHAT YOU'LL NEED

TEMPLATE PLASTIC

X-ACTO® KNIFE

Self-healing CUTTING MAT

STENCIL BRUSH

Leaf Stenciling

Step 1 Trace stencil onto template plastic.

Step 2 Lay the template plastic on the self-healing cutting mat. Using an X-Acto® knife, cut out the stencil design.

Step 3 With the dry brush technique (see below) stencil design onto walls, working from the outside of the design to the inside.

Step 4 Turn leaf design randomly for an all-over pattern or stencil in rows for a stripe variation.

Dry Brush Technique

Step 1 Pour a small amount of paint onto a disposable coated plate.

Step 2 Dip tip of the dry stencil brush into paint.

Step 3 Wipe off excess paint on a paper towel until brush is "dry." Do this by pouncing the brush in an up and down motion to evenly distribute the paint and rid it of excess paint.

Step 4 Place stencil on the surface to be stenciled and hold the brush perpendicular to the stencil.

Step 5 Using a gentle circular motion, work around the edges of the stencil to the inside. Generally, stencils have lighter centers than edges, giving the design some highlights and interest. Reload the brush as necessary. Always remember to wipe off excess paint and continue to work with a "dry" brush.

There are stencil adhesive sprays available that help hold the edges of the stencil securely to the surface. Follow manufacturer's instructions.

Leaf Stencil
Template

CHRISTMAS
by the fire

*Take a break from the hectic pace of the holidays with a
candlelight evening for two spent relaxing in front
of the fire. Experience the quiet with a friend or
spouse and discover the true rewards of rest and relaxation.*

Christmas by the fire

Creating a quiet haven can be as simple as pulling a small table and chairs close to the fireplace. Lynette adds to the warmth by tossing a quilt over the table and filling the chairs with soft comforts—an antique quilt and her Patchwork Blossom Pillow shown on the previous page.

KEEP THE CANDLE BURNING. The flames of friendship will burn longer and brighter if tended on a regular basis. Even during the busy holidays, take the time to "sit for a spell." Here, the centerpiece is a flowerpot painted cream, filled with dried hydrangeas, Spanish moss, berries and a candle protected by a glass cylinder.

BRIGHT COLORS TURN DREAR INTO CHEER. Even tea for two or a simple soup supper can be a special occasion with the right tabletop accessories. Lynete starts with a vintage quilt pieced to look like a red brick fireplace. To replicate this antique quilt, use solid red fabric for bricks and muslin for morter strips. The brick pieces should be cut 4-1/2-inches x 8-1/2-inches and the muslin morter strips should be cut 1-inch wide. Using 1/4-inch seam allowances, assemble blocks in a staggered brick fashion. This quilt has no borders. Bind with muslin following the binding instructions in the General Instructions.

The checked napkin with binding is shown on page 45 and is 16-1/2 inches square.

WHAT YOU'LL NEED

Makes 4 napkins

Yardage is based on 42-inch wide fabric

1 yard GREEN CHECK
for napkin tops

1-5/8 yards GREEN PRINT
for napkin backs and binding

Napkins

Cutting

From GREEN CHECK:
- Cut 4, 16-1/2-inch squares

From GREEN PRINT:
- Cut 4, 16-1/2-inch squares
- Cut 8, 2-3/4 x 42-inch binding strips

Piecing

Step 1   With wrong sides together, sew the 16-1/2-inch GREEN CHECK and GREEN PRINT squares together in pairs, a scant 1/4-inch from the raw edges.

Step 2   Stitch diagonally from corner to corner to stabilize each napkin.

Step 3   Diagonally piece the 2-3/4-inch wide GREEN PRINT binding strips together as needed. Sew the binding to each napkin using a 3/8-inch seam allowance. This measurement will produce a 1/2-inch wide finished double binding. Refer to page 139 for Binding and Diagonal Piecing Instructions.

The Patchwork Blossom Pillow is shown on page 45 and measures 16-inches square without the ruffle.

WHAT YOU'LL NEED

Yardage is based on 42-inch wide fabric

5-1/2 x 16-inch piece RED PRINT for block

1-3/8 yards DARK GREEN PRINT for block, border, ruffle, and pillow back

4 x 16-inch piece MEDIUM GREEN PRINT for block

7 x 42-inch strip BEIGE PRINT for background

16-inch pillow form

Pillow Front

Cutting

From RED PRINT:
- Cut 1, 4-1/2-inch square
- Cut 4, 2-1/2-inch squares

From DARK GREEN PRINT:
- Cut 2, 2-1/2 x 42-inch border strips
- Cut 4, 2-1/2-inch squares
- Cut 4, 2-1/2 x 4-1/2-inch rectangles

From MEDIUM GREEN PRINT:
- Cut 4, 2-7/8-inch squares

From BEIGE PRINT:
- Cut 4, 2-7/8-inch squares
- Cut 8, 2-1/2-inch squares
- Cut 4, 2-1/2 x 4-1/2-inch rectangles

Piecing

Step 1   Layer the 2-7/8-inch MEDIUM GREEN and BEIGE squares together in pairs. Cut the layered squares in half diagonally to make 8 sets of triangles. Stitch 1/4-inch from the diagonal edge of each set of triangles, and press.

Make 8, 2-1/2-inch triangle-pieced squares

Step 2   Sew the 2-1/2-inch RED squares to 4 of the triangle-pieced squares, and press.

Make 4

Sew the 2-1/2-inch DARK GREEN squares to 4 of the triangle-pieced squares, and press. Sew these units together in pairs, and press.

Step 3   Position a 2-1/2-inch BEIGE square on the corner of a 2-1/2 x 4-1/2-inch DARK GREEN

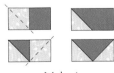

Make 4

rectangle. Draw a diagonal line on the BEIGE square and stitch on the line. Trim the seam allowance to 1/4-inch, and press. Repeat this process at the opposite corner of the DARK GREEN rectangle.

Step 4 Sew a 2-1/2 x 4-1/2-inch BEIGE rectangle to the bottom of a Step 3 unit, and press.

Make 4

Step 5 Sew Step 2 units to both sides of 2 of the Step 4 units, and press.

Make 2

Step 6 Sew 2 of the Step 4 units to the top and bottom edges of the 4-1/2-inch RED square and press. Sew the Step 5 units to the sides of the block, and press. At this point the block should measure 12-1/2-inches square.

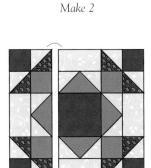

Step 7 To attach the 2-1/2-inch wide DARK GREEN border strips, refer to page 138 for Border Instructions.

Pillow Ruffle

Cutting

From DARK GREEN PRINT:
- Cut 4, 5-1/2 x 42-inch strips

Attaching the Ruffle

Step 1 Diagonally piece the 5-1/2-inch wide DARK GREEN strips together to make a continuous ruffle strip, referring to page 139 for Diagonal Piecing Instructions.

Step 2 Fold the strip in half lengthwise, wrong sides together, and press. Divide the ruffle strip into 4 equal segments, and mark the quarter points with safety pins.

Step 3 To gather the ruffle, position a heavy-weight thread (or 2 strands of regular weight sewing thread) 1/4-inch in from the raw edges of the folded ruffle.

Secure   *Zigzag*

Note: *You will need a length of heavyweight thread 130-inches long. Secure one end of the thread by stitching across it. Zigzag-stitch over the thread all the way around the ruffle, taking care not to sew through it.*

Step 4 With right sides together, pin the ruffle to the pillow front, matching the quarter points of the ruffle to the corners of the pillow front. Pull up the gathering stitches until the ruffle fits the pillow front, taking care to allow extra fullness in the ruffle at each corner. Sew the ruffle to the pillow front, using a 1/4-inch seam allowance.

Pillow Back

Cutting

From DARK GREEN PRINT:
- Cut 2, 16-1/2 x 21-inch rectangles

Assembling the Pillow Back

Step 1 With wrong sides together, fold the 2, 16-1/2 x 21-inch DARK GREEN rectangles in half to form 2, 10-1/2 x 16-1/2-inch double-thick pillow back pieces. Overlap the 2 folded edges by about 4-inches so the pillow back measures 16-1/2-inches square, and pin. Stitch around the entire piece to create a single pillow back, using a 1/4-inch seam allowance.

Step 2 With right sides together, layer the pillow back and the pillow front, and pin. The ruffle will be turned toward the center of the pillow at this time. Stitch around the outside edges using a 1/2-inch seam allowance.

Step 3 Trim the pillow back and corner seam allowances if needed. Turn the pillow right side out and fluff up the ruffle. Insert the pillow form through the back opening.

Overlap

Fold

Christmas for kids

*Even though Lynette's children are grown up, she finds it fun
to treat her guests (young and old alike) to a room filled with
Christmas treats for the kid in all of us. She designed the
window treatments, bedding, quilts and pillows using fabric
from her Kids Under Cover collection for Thimbleberries®.*

Scottie Dog Quilt

The Scottie Dog Quilt is shown on page 51 and measures 70-inches square.

WHAT YOU'LL NEED

The following fabrics and supplies are needed to duplicate this antique quilt

Yardage is based on 42-inch wide fabric

5-3/4 yards MUSLIN for appliqué foundation, alternate blocks, and side and corner triangles

10-inch squares of 25 Assorted MEDIUM PRINTS for Scottie dog appliqués

2/3 yard RED PRINT for binding

4-1/4 yards Backing Fabric

Quilt Batting, at least 75-inches square

3 yards Freezer Paper for appliqué

5 packages of Assorted Colors of 1/2-inch wide bias tape

Black embroidery Floss for decorative stitches

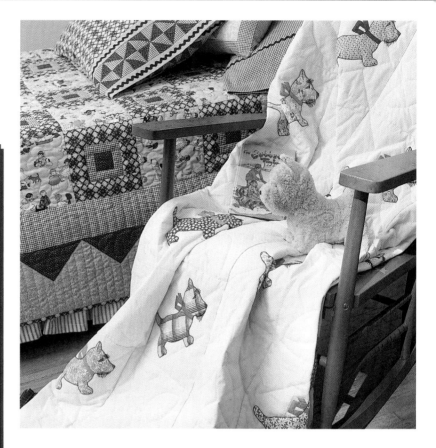

Scottie Dog Blocks (Make 25)

Cutting

From MUSLIN:

- Cut 7, 10-1/2 x 42-inch strips.
  You may need to cut additional strips.
  From these strips cut:
  25, 10-1/2-inch appliqué foundation squares

Appliqué the Scottie Dogs
(Freezer Paper Technique)

Note: With this method of hand appliqué, the freezer paper forms a base around which each Scottie dog is shaped.

Step 1 Lay a piece of freezer paper, paper side up, over the Scottie dog shape, and use a pencil to trace this shape 25 times. Cut out the Scottie dog on the traced lines.

Step 2 With a dry iron on the wool setting, press the coated side of each freezer paper Scottie dog onto the wrong side of the Assorted Medium Print squares. If cutting more than one Scottie dog from a particular print, allow at least 1/2-inch between each shape for seam allowances.

Step 3 Cut out each Scottie dog a scant 1/4-inch beyond the edge of the freezer paper pattern. Finger-press the seam allowance over the edge of the freezer paper.

Step 4 Referring to the block diagram, center a Scottie dog, on-point, on a 10-1/2-inch Muslin square.

Step 5 To make the bow appliqué, refer to the appliqué pattern for placement. Position a 5-inch section of bias tape on the 10-1/2-inch Muslin appliqué square, mitering the corners and tucking the ends under the Scottie dog and stitch in place with matching thread. Then position a 2-inch section of bias tape on the square, angling the upper end (turning under 1/8-inch) and tucking the opposite end under the Scottie dog. With matching thread, stitch the strip in place. Position a 2-1/2-inch section of bias tape on the neck, turning the ends under the Scottie dog and stitch in place with matching thread.

Step 6 Appliqué the Scottie dog to the Muslin square with matching thread. When there is about 3/4-inch left to appliqué, slide your needle into this opening and loosen the freezer paper. Gently remove it, and finish stitching the Scottie dog in place. Repeat to make a total of 25 appliqué blocks.

Step 7 Referring to page 55 for details, with 3 strands of black embroidery, outline stitch around the Scottie dog shape and the facial features. Refer to page 139 for decorative stitch diagrams.

Quilt Center

Note: *The side and corner triangles are larger than necessary and will be trimmed before the binding is added.*

Cutting

From MUSLIN:
- Cut 2, 16 x 42-inch strips.
  From these strips cut:
  4, 16-inch squares. Cut the squares diagonally into quarters for a total of 16 side triangles.

- Cut 4, 10-1/2 x 42-inch strips. You may need to cut additional strips.
  From these strips cut:
  16, 10-1/2-inch squares for alternate blocks
- Cut 1, 10 x 42-inch strip.
  From this strip cut:
  2, 10-inch squares. Cut the squares in half diagonally for a total of 4 corner triangles.

Assembling the Quilt Center

Step 1 Referring to the quilt diagram, lay out the Scottie dog blocks and the 10-1/2-inch Muslin alternate blocks. Sew the pieces together in diagonal rows. Press the seam allowances in alternating directions by rows so the seams will fit snugly together with less bulk.

Step 2 Pin the rows at the block intersections and sew the rows together. Press the seam allowances in one direction.

Step 3 Sew the Muslin corner triangles to the quilt, and press.

Step 4 Trim away the excess fabric from the side and corner triangles, taking care to allow a 1/4-inch seam allowance beyond the corners of each block. Refer to Trimming Side and Corner Triangles on page 140.

Putting It All Together

Cut the 4-1/4 yard length of backing fabric in half crosswise to make 2, 2-1/8 yard lengths. Refer to Finishing the Quilt on page 139 for complete instructions.

Binding

Cutting

From RED PRINT:
- Cut 8, 2-3/4 x 42-inch strips

Sew the binding to the quilt using a 3/8-inch seam allowance. This measurement will produce a 1/2-inch wide finished double binding. Refer to page 139 for Binding and Diagonal Piecing Instructions.

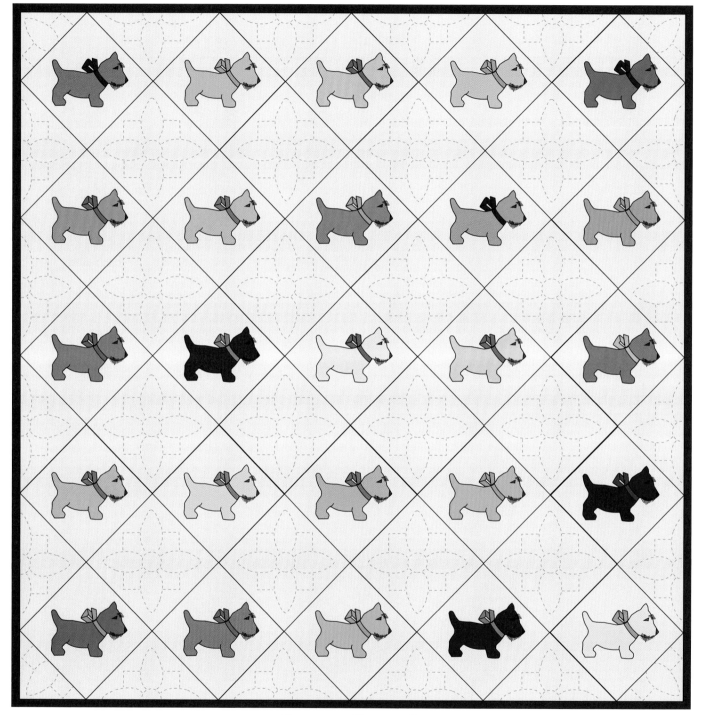

Scottie Dog Quilt

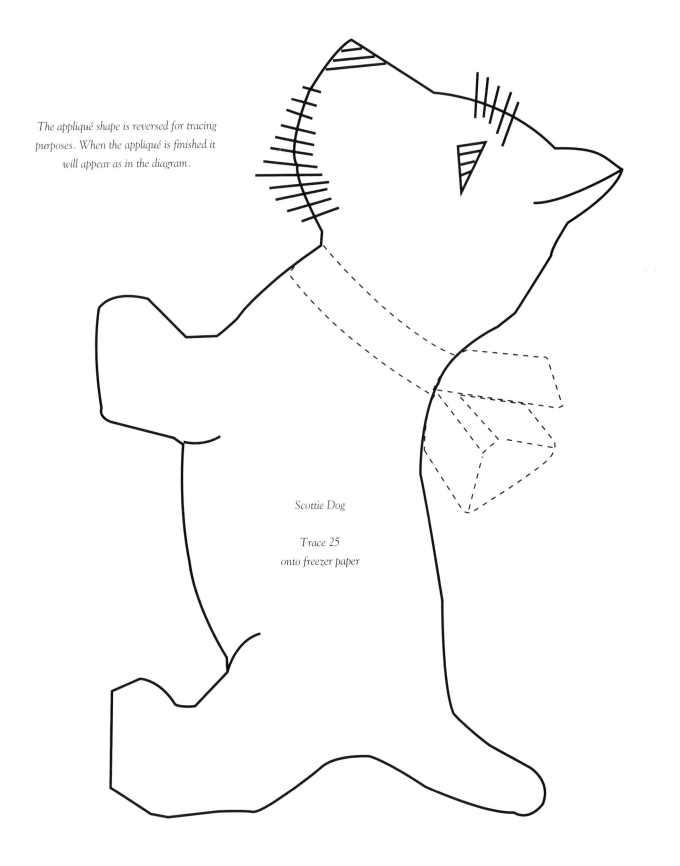

The appliqué shape is reversed for tracing purposes. When the appliqué is finished it will appear as in the diagram.

Scottie Dog

Trace 25
onto freezer paper

The Pinwheel and Rickrack Pillowcases shown here measure 19-3/4 x 31-3/4 inches.

WHAT YOU'LL NEED

Yardage is based on 42-inch wide fabric

7/8 yard BLUE/RED GRID
for pillowcase

1/4 yard RED PRINT
for pinwheels

1/4 yard RED CHECK
for pinwheels

3/8 yard BLUE PRINT
for cuff borders and facing

1 package jumbo rickrack for trim

**Standard Bed Pillow
(20 x 26-inches)**

Pinwheel Pillowcase

Cutting

From BLUE/RED GRID:
- Cut 2, 20-1/2 x 26-1/2-inch rectangles

From RED PRINT:
- Cut 2, 2-7/8 x 42-inch strips

From RED CHECK:
- Cut 2, 2-7/8 x 42-inch strips

From BLUE PRINT:
- Cut 2, 2 x 42-inch strips.
  From these strips cut:
  4, 2 x 20-1/2-inch border strips
- Cut 1, 7-1/2 x 42-inch strip for cuff facing

Pinwheel Blocks (Make 10)

Step 1   With right sides together, layer the 2-7/8 x 42-inch RED PRINT strips and RED CHECK strips in pairs. Press together, but do not sew. Cut the layered strips into 20 squares. Cut the layered squares in half diagonally to make 40 sets of triangles. Stitch 1/4-inch from the diagonal edge of each pair of triangles, and press. At this point each triangle-pieced square should measure 2-1/2-inches square.

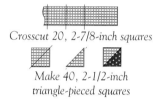
Crosscut 20, 2-7/8-inch squares

Make 40, 2-1/2-inch triangle-pieced squares

Step 2   Sew the triangle-pieced squares together in pairs, and press. Sew the pairs together to form the pinwheel block. At this point each pinwheel block should measure 4-1/2-inches square.

Make 20

Make 10

Step 3   Sew 5 of the pinwheel blocks together for each cuff, and press. At this point each pinwheel strip should measure 4-1/2 x 20-1/2-inches.

Step 4 Sew a 2 x 20-1/2-inch BLUE strip to both long edges of each pinwheel strip, and press.

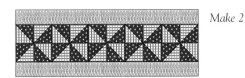

Make 2

Step 5 Sew the Step 4 pinwheel strips to each 20-1/2 x 26-1/2-inch BLUE/RED GRID rectangle, and press. Sew the pillowcase sections together along one long edge, and press. Center the rickrack down the center of each BLUE border. Keep in mind you will need a 1/4-inch seam allowance at the top edge of the upper BLUE border. With matching thread, zigzag stitch the rickrack in place.

Step 6 Add the 7-1/2 x 42-inch BLUE cuff facing strip to the top edge of the pillowcase using a 1/4-inch seam allowance, and press. Press under 1/4-inch along the opposite long edge. Press the facing to the back side of the cuff and topstitch in place.

Facing

Turn under 1/4-inch and press

Step 7 With right sides together, fold the pillowcase in half and sew the side and bottom raw edges together using a 1/2-inch seam allowance. Turn the pillowcase right side out and insert the pillow.

Rickrack Pillowcase

Fabrics and Supplies for one standard pillowcase

19-3/4 x 31-3/4-inches
Yardage is based on 42-inch wide fabric

1-1/4 yards RED CHECK for pillowcase

1 package of jumbo Rickrack for trim

Standard Bed Pillow (20 x 26-inches)

Assemble the Pillowcase

Step 1 Measure the distance around the middle of your pillow, and add 1-inch to the measurement to allow for a 1/2-inch seam allowance. Measure the length of your pillow, and add 13-inches to the measurement to allow for a 1/2-inch seam allowance at one end and a hem at the other end.

Step 2 Cut a RED CHECK rectangle according to the measurements determined in Step 1.

Step 3 Turn one long edge under 1/2-inch, and press. Turn the same edge under 6-inches, and press. Topstitch in place.

Step 4 Position the rickrack on the topstitching line. With matching thread, zigzag-stitch the rickrack in place.

Step 5 With right sides together, fold the hemmed rectangle in half and sew the raw edges together using a 1/2-inch seam 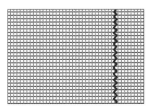 allowance. Turn the pillowcase right side out and insert the pillow.

The Kids Around the Block Quilt is shown on page 51 and measures 80 x 96 inches.

WHAT YOU'LL NEED

Yardage is based on 42-inch wide fabric

1-1/2 yards RED PRINT
for blocks and dogtooth border

1-5/8 yards BLUE CHECK
for blocks and inner border

1-3/4 yards BLUE/RED/BEIGE PLAID for blocks

2 yards LARGE BEIGE PRINT
for alternate blocks

2-1/2 yards LIGHT RED PRINT
for dogtooth border and outer border

7/8 yard BLUE/RED/BEIGE PLAID
for binding

5-3/4 yards Backing Fabric

Quilt Batting,
at least 84 x 100-inches

Pieced Blocks (Make 32)

Cutting

From RED PRINT:
- Cut 2, 2-1/2 x 42-inch strips

From BLUE CHECK:
- Cut 4, 1-1/2 x 42-inch strips
- Cut 8 more 1-1/2 x 42-inch strips.
  From these strips cut:
  64, 1-1/2 x 4-1/2-inch rectangles

From BLUE/RED/BEIGE PLAID:
- Cut 23, 2-1/2 x 42-inch strips.
  From these strips cut:
  64, 2-1/2 x 4-1/2-inch rectangles
  64, 2-1/2 x 8-1/2-inch rectangles

Piecing

Step 1 Aligning long edges, sew 1-1/2 x 42-inch BLUE CHECK strips to both sides of a 2-1/2 x 42-inch RED strip, and press. Repeat to make 2 strip sets. Cut the strip sets into segments.

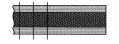

Crosscut 32, 2-1/2-inch wide segments

Step 2 Sew 1-1/2 x 4-1/2-inch BLUE CHECK rectangles to both sides of a Step 1 unit, and press.

Make 32

Step 3 Sew 2-1/2 x 4-1/2-inch BLUE/RED/BEIGE PLAID rectangles to the top and bottom of the Step 2 unit, and press. Sew 2-1/2 x 8-1/2-inch BLUE/RED/BEIGE PLAID rectangles to both sides of the unit and press.

Make 32

At this point each block should measure 8-1/2-inches square.

Quilt Center

Cutting

From LARGE BEIGE PRINT:
- Cut 8, 8-1/2 x 42-inch strips.
  From these strips cut:
  31, 8-1/2-inch squares for alternate blocks

Assembly

Step 1 Referring to the quilt diagram for placement, lay out the pieced blocks and alternate blocks in 9 horizontal rows of 7 blocks each. Sew the blocks together in rows. Press the seam allowances toward the LARGE BEIGE PRINT alternate blocks.

Step 2 Pin the rows at the block intersections and sew the rows together. Press the seam allowances in one direction.

Borders

Note: The yardage given allows for the border strips to be cut on the crosswise grain. Diagonally piece the strips as needed, referring to page 139 for Diagonal Piecing Instructions.

Cutting

From BLUE CHECK:
- Cut 7, 4-1/2 x 42-inch inner border strips

From RED PRINT:
- Cut 8, 4-1/2 x 42-inch strips.
  From these strips cut:
  32, 4-1/2 x 8-1/2-inch rectangles
- Cut 4, 4-7/8-inch squares

From LIGHT RED PRINT:
- Cut 9, 4-1/2 x 42-inch outer border strips
- Cut 8, 4-1/2 x 42-inch strips.
  From these strips cut:
  68, 4-1/2-inch squares
- Cut 4, 4-7/8-inch squares

Attaching the Borders

Step 1 To attach the 4-1/2-inch wide BLUE CHECK inner border strips, refer to page 138 for Border Instructions.

Step 2 Position a 4-1/2-inch LIGHT RED square on the corner of a 4-1/2 x 8-1/2-inch RED PRINT rectangle. Draw a diagonal line on the LIGHT RED square, and stitch on the line. Trim the seam allowance to 1/4-inch, and press. Repeat this process at the opposite corner of the RED PRINT rectangle.

Make 32 dogtooth units

Step 3 Layer together a 4-7/8-inch LIGHT RED square and a 4-7/8-inch RED PRINT square. Cut the layered square in half diagonally to make 2 sets of triangles. Stitch 1/4-inch from the diagonal edge of each set of triangles, and press. Repeat with the remaining 4-7/8-inch LIGHT RED and RED PRINT squares. At this point each triangle-pieced square should measure 4-1/2-inches square.

Make 8, 4-1/2-inch triangle-pieced squares

Step 4 For the top and bottom dogtooth borders, sew together 7 of the Step 2 dogtooth units and 2 of the Step 3 triangle-pieced squares, and press. Sew the dogtooth border strips to the quilt center, and press.

Step 5 For the side dogtooth borders, sew together 9 of the Step 2 dogtooth units and 2 of the Step 3 triangle-pieced squares, and press. Add 4-1/2-inch LIGHT RED PRINT squares to both ends of the border strips and press. Sew the dogtooth border strips to the quilt center, and press.

Step 6 To attach the 4-1/2-inch wide LIGHT RED outer border strips, refer to page 138 for Border Instructions.

Putting It All Together

Cut the 5-3/4 yard length of backing fabric in half crosswise to form 2, 2-7/8 yard lengths. Refer to Finishing the Quilt on page 139 for complete instructions.

Binding

Cutting

From BLUE/RED/BEIGE PLAID:
- Cut 10, 2-3/4 x 42-inch strips

Sew the binding to the quilt using a 3/8-inch seam allowance. This measurement will produce a 1/2-inch wide finished double binding. Refer to page 139 for Binding and Diagonal Piecing Instructions.

Kids Around The Block Quilt

Christmas for kids

When it comes to decorating trees for Christmas, Lynette gets plenty of practice. She feels that the sight and scent of a fresh evergreen tree is like a little bit of holiday heaven for every room in the house. Kids will think so too, especially when the tree is loaded with lollipops and just waiting to be discovered in a child's bedroom!

VISIONS OF SUGARPLUMS. What could be more fun for a kid than a treat-filled lollipop tree? Start with a garland of Grapenut O's® Cereal strung on twine, add bundles of jumbo crayons, and then in the branches nestle edible ornaments such as Safety® Suckers and sugar cookies with Teddy Grahams® secured with frosting.

TOP OFF THE TOY BOX. For a fresh approach to a standard-issue toy box, Lynette trims the sides with a border of decoupaged pages from a child's storybook, and tops it off with the short, but sweet, lollipop tree.

Christmas for kids

Half the fun of creating a kid-friendly room is filling it with treasures from yesteryear. Personalize it with toys, Teddy bears, and books that bring fond memories of Christmas past to Christmas present.

ALL DECKED OUT. Playtime from the past takes on new interest with an antique toy chalkboard (missing the chalkboard) holding a collection of antique flashcards and charming children's books. Below, Teddies of all shapes and sizes take over the playroom. For more display space, go up instead of out by using tall bookshelves or stacking vintage benches one atop the other for a pyramid of fun!

Pinwheel Stocking

The Pinwheel Stocking is shown on page 63 and measures 17-1/2 inches long.

WHAT YOU'LL NEED

Yardage is based on 42-inch wide fabric

5/8 yard DARK RED PRINT for pinwheels and stocking back

1/4 yard RED CHECK for pinwheels

1/3 yard BEIGE PRINT for pinwheels

3-1/2 x 42-inch strip BLUE/RED GRID for binding and hanger

1/2 yard MUSLIN for lining

PELLON® FLEECE, at least 14 x 42-inches

10, 1/2-inch diameter Buttons

Optional: 8-inch length of rickrack for hanger

Stocking Front Assembly

Pinwheel Blocks

    Make 10 DARK RED PRINT pinwheel blocks

    Make 10 RED CHECK pinwheel blocks

Cutting

From DARK RED PRINT:
- Cut 2, 2-3/8 x 42-inch strips

From RED CHECK:
- Cut 2, 2-3/8 x 42-inch strips

From BEIGE PRINT:
- Cut 4, 2-3/8 x 42-inch strips

Piecing

Step 1   With right sides together, layer the 2-3/8 x 42-inch DARK RED PRINT strips and 2 of the BEIGE strips in pairs. Press together, but do not sew. Cut the layered strips into squares. Cut the layered squares in half diagonally to make 40 sets of triangles. Stitch 1/4-inch from the diagonal edge of each pair of triangles, and press. At this point each triangle-pieced square should measure 2-inches square.

Crosscut 20, 2-3/8-inch squares

Make 40, 2-inch triangle-pieced squares

Step 2   Sew the triangle-pieced squares together in pairs, and press. Sew the pairs together to make pinwheel Block A. At this point each pinwheel block should measure 3-1/2-inches square.

Make 20

Block A Make 10

Step 3   In the same manner, make 10 RED CHECK and BEIGE Block B pinwheel blocks. At this point each pinwheel block should measure 3-1/2-inches square.

Make 20

Block B
Make 10

Step 4 Referring to the diagram for placement, sew the Block A and Block B pinwheels together in 6 rows. Press the seam allowances toward the A Blocks. Sew the rows together, and press the seam allowances in one direction.

Step 5 Refer to Basic Stocking Assembly Instructions, below, to complete the stocking.

Basic Stocking Assembly

Cutting

From Stocking Back fabric:
- Cut 1, 14 x 20-inch rectangle for stocking back

From Muslin Lining and Pellon® Fleece:
- Cut 2, 14 x 20-inch rectangles of each

From Binding/Hanger fabric:
- Cut 1, 2-3/4 x 16-inch binding strip
- Cut 1, 1-3/4 x 8-inch hanger strip

Assembling the Stocking Front

Step 1 Position the stocking pattern on the stocking front and cut out.

Step 2 Layer together one muslin lining rectangle, one fleece rectangle, and the stocking front (facing up). Baste the 3 layers together and quilt as desired.

Step 3 Baste around the stocking front, 1/4-inch from the edges. Trim the muslin lining and fleece even with the raw edges of the stocking front.

Muslin lining ↓   Pellon® Fleece

Assembling the Stocking Back

Note: Do not cut the stocking shape from the fabric designated for the stocking back. The technique that follows treats the stocking back as a rectangular unit of layered fabric and batting. It is much easier and more accurate than trying to align so many layers and cut edges.

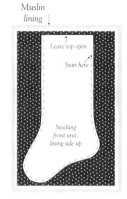

Muslin lining ↓

Leave top open

Start here

Stocking front unit, lining side up

Step 1 Layer together the remaining muslin lining rectangle and fleece rectangle, and the stocking back rectangle (facing up). Baste the 3 layers together.

Step 2 Lay the stocking front unit (lining side up) on top of the stocking back unit (lining side down). Pin the units together (with right sides facing) and stitch together with a 1/4-inch seam allowance, leaving the top edge open.

Step 3 Trim the backing, fleece, and lining even with the stocking front. Turn the stocking right side out.

Step 4 Sew the buttons in the center of the pinwheels.

Hanger and Top Binding

Step 1 With wrong sides together, fold the long edges of the 1-3/4 x 8-inch hanger strip toward each other so that they will meet at the center.

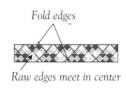

Fold edges

Raw edges meet in center

Step 2 Fold the strip in half lengthwise once more, and stitch the folded edges together to make a hanger strip approximately 1/2 x 8-inches.

Step 3 Fold the hanger strip (or rickrack) in half crosswise and position it on the outside of the stocking at the center back seam line, aligning the raw edges. Baste the hanger in place.

Step 4 With wrong sides together, fold the 2-3/4 x 16-inch binding strip in half lengthwise. With raw edges even, bind the top edge of the stocking, referring to page 139 for Binding and Diagonal Piecing Instructions.

Stocking Toe
Pattern

Cut 1

Stocking Front
Pattern

Cut 1

Christmas for kids

In this bedroom, Lynette stenciled a charming checkerboard border to trim the walls and tie the room together.

EYE-CATCHING ACCENTS. A checkerboard wall stencil and matching valances on the windows above the bed (see page 51) and the desk pull the eye around the room. For color and texture, the valance is trimmed with second and third fabrics added to the top and bottom. Valance and curtains simply gather on wooden rods.

BACK BY POPULAR DEMAND. Lynette takes special joy in preserving pieces of the past. Novel uses for castaways include a child's toy xylophone reborn as a table lamp. A toy top and vintage wood cutouts of children surrounded by greens add to the arrangement.

CHRISTMAS
outdoors

Welcome friends and family with Christmas
greetings that begin even before they reach
the front door. Guests are twice blessed upon their
arrival at Lynette's Christmas cottage—
the inviting greens and holiday decorations all
around the outside of the house are a promise of the
warmth and welcome that await just inside the door.

Christmas outdoors

To extend a warm welcome outdoors as well as indoors, gather armloads of greens, berries, twigs and pine cones and arrange them artfully at the entrance to your holiday home.

NATURE'S BOUNTY BECKONS. Let nature provide all you need for making a holiday decorating statement by the wagon-load—right in your own front yard. Lynette finds that making memorable decorations requires more imagination than time or money. Here, she fills an old painted wine barrel and buggy with greens, rose hip, crab apple, and red twig dogwood branches.

NATURAL ELEMENTS ARE ESSENTIAL. A rustic twig chair is host to nature's finest holiday assortment in an old painted bushel basket. To enhance the appearance of abundance, Lynette fills the front flower bed with small tree tops before the ground freezes in Minnesota.

Christmas outdoors

Lynette uses gifts from the garden to create unique outdoor arrangements that spread Christmas cheer throughout the yard and are a welcome sight for the neighbors.

GIVE IT A SPRINKLING OF HOLIDAY SPIRIT. Lynette puts the watering can to work all winter long by filling it with fresh greens, red twig dogwood and dried hydrangea blossoms from her garden.

SCOOP UP SOME SEASONS GREETINGS. Even the potting shed digs in to greet the season with an eye-catching arrangement of greens, white-frosted pine cones, and a well-used shovel.

SHED SOME CHEER. A drying screen hung with a wreath, swag, and antique red lantern brightens the space next to the potting shed door.

Snow Candle

The snow candle shown here is about 16-inches inches tall.

WHAT YOU'LL NEED

3 to 4-inch thick LOG ROUNDS

GLASS HURRICANE

RICE PAPER

RAFFIA

GREENS, artificial BERRIES and PINE CONES

Small WREATH (artificial will work)

Assembling

Step 1 Cut the rice paper to fit the glass hurricane. Wrap around the hurricane.

Step 2 Wrap raffia around the hurricane and tie to secure rice paper and tie into a bow.

Step 3 Place a few sprigs of berries and pine greens under raffia bow.

Step 4 Embellish the wreath as desired.

Step 5 Place the wreath on log round. Place the candle inside the hurricane. When lighted, the rice paper will make the entire hurricane glow.

CHRISTMAS on the porch

Rustic by day and romantic by candlelight, the porch is the perfect place for country cottage-style Christmas decorating and entertaining. Early in the day, Lynette prepares the table on the porch for evening guests who will see it sparkling with holiday splendor.

Christmas on the porch

Christmas on the porch clearly calls for decorating with forest hues and naturals, but Lynette adds a sophisticated symphony of cream and black to the table setting for a touch of elegance. The table setting shown here is the dessert portion of a progressive dinner. For a special presentation, Lynette serves generous helpings of apple cranberry cobbler with cinnamon ice cream in large, flat soup bowls with wide rims.

A STUDY IN CONTRAST. For the table, Lynette bordered a cream tablecloth with blocks of deep shades of brown, red, and black print fabric. Cream accents include the painted flower pot and wooden candlesticks. The hint of stencil pattern beneath the table is a section of the porch floor which has been entirely painted to replicate a quilt.

PLACE CARDS ARE A WELCOME SIGHT. Guests feel special when they find reserved places at the table. Various layers of textured paper in colors to match the table setting are topped with a rubber stamped pine cone colored to look like an old-fashioned sepia print. For a touch of holiday sparkle, the complementary pine cone decoration is frosted with gold paint.

For Filling:

6 CUPS PEELED AND SLICED APPLES

I CUP RAW CRANBERRIES

I CUP SUGAR

4 T. FLOUR

1/4 TSP. GROUND CINNAMON

For Cobbler Crust:

1-1/3 CUP FLOUR

3/4 TSP. BAKING POWDER

1/2 TSP. SALT

1/4 TSP. BAKING SODA

1-1/2 T. VEGETABLE OIL

I T. CHILLED BUTTER CUT

INTO SMALL PIECES

1/3 CUP SOUR CREAM

4 T. MILK

For Glaze:

I EGG, SLIGHTLY BEATEN

2 T. SUGAR

Grease a 3-quart baking dish. Combine apples, cranberries, 1 cup sugar, 4 T. flour, and cinnamon. Spread evenly in the greased baking dish.

To prepare the cobbler crust, combine 1-1/3 cup flour, baking powder, salt and baking soda. Work in oil and butter until coarse crumbs form. In a large bowl, whisk sour cream and milk. Add flour mixture and stir with a fork just until a dough forms. On a lightly floured surface, roll out dough approximately 1/2-inch smaller than the baking dish. Place dough onto the filling. Cut several small cuts in dough to vent steam. Brush top with egg and sprinkle with 2 T. sugar.

Bake 40 minutes at 375 degrees or until top is golden brown, filling is bubbling, and a toothpick inserted in the center comes out clean. Cool for at least 10 minutes. Serve warm with cinnamon or vanilla ice cream.

Serves 8–10.

Christmas on the porch

Lynette finds the porch the perfect place to display a variety of collectibles featuring Christmas colors and themes. Unusual display surfaces include a plank top table and a vintage tin picnic basket.

HOMEMADE BUT HANDSOME. Nestled under a framed Santa's sleigh (formerly a store display) the antique house with vintage lights brightens a corner of the cottage porch.

NOW YOU CAN SEE THE FOREST FOR THE TREES. Lynette's collection of bottle brush trees make a statement when grouped. To create a forest of bottle brush trees, fill a metal pan painted red with florist foam. Work from the center out, securing each tree with a U-shaped florist pin at the base of the tree. Pack the trees closely together, keeping the larger trees in the center and adding the smaller trees to the outer rim. Finish by covering the foam with sphagnum moss.

Christmas on the porch

Small decorations like the candle bundles and the appliqué runner add nostalgic charm to tabletops. They are also great for gift-giving. Make up several ahead of the holiday rush to have on hand for quick gifts.

UP AND RUNNING IN PLENTY OF TIME FOR THE HOLIDAYS. Lynette combines houses, hearts, holly, and a gingerbread man in a block-bordered table runner that works up quickly. Make it in multiples for gifts.

SHARE SYMBOLS OF THE SEASON. For a useful holiday gift, bundle up cream-colored candles with an antique postcard tied together with narrow ribbon. In the background, a twig easel holds a vintage chalk winter scene still in its original frame.

The Holiday Table Topper is shown on page 81 and measures 24 x 40-inches.

What you'll need

Yardage is based on 42-inch wide fabric

3/4 yard RED PRINT for runner center and pieced border

3/8 yard GREEN PRINT for pieced border

3/4 yard BLACK PRINT for appliqué backing, inner border, and corner squares

3/8 yard BLACK PRINT for binding

7/8 yard Backing Fabric

2 yards Paper-backed Fusible Web

#8 Black pearl cotton or embroidery floss for decorative stitches

Quilt Batting at least 28 x 44-inches

Additional fabrics needed for appliqués

1 Ginger House
   7-inch square BROWN PRINT
   3-inch square RED PRINT for heart
   3 x 6-inch rectangle BLACK/
   BROWN PRINT for chimney/door

A Pair of Hearts
   6-inch square MEDIUM RED PRINT
   6-inch square DARK RED PRINT

3 Holly Berries
   5-inch square RED PRINT

3 Holly Leaves
   8-inch square GREEN PRINT

1 Gingerbread Man
   9-inch square BROWN PRINT

Appliqué the Runner Center

Cutting

From RED PRINT:
- Cut 1, 12-1/2 x 28-1/2-inch rectangle

From BLACK PRINT, backing fabric and fusible web cut:
- 1, 9-inch square of each for the pair of hearts
- 1, 8-inch square of each for the ginger house
- 1, 5-inch square of each for the 3 holly berries
- 1, 8-inch square of each for the holly leaves
- 1, 9-inch square of each for the gingerbread man

Fusible Web Appliqué

Step 1 Trace the appliqué shapes on the paper side of the remaining fusible web, leaving 1/2-inch between each shape. Cut the shapes apart, leaving a small margin beyond the drawn lines.

Note: When you are fusing a large shape like the gingerbread man, fuse just the outer edges of the shape, so that it will not look stiff when finished. To do this, draw a line about 3/8-inch inside the shape, and cut away the fusible web on this line, as shown below.

Step 2 Following the manufacturer's instructions, apply the fusible web shapes to the wrong side of the fabrics chosen for the appliqués. Let the fabrics cool and cut on the traced line. Peel off the paper backing.

Step 3 Center the prepared appliqué shapes on the corresponding BLACK PRINT squares. Referring to the diagrams, layer the chimney under the roofline of the house, and layer the large heart under the right edge of the medium heart. With a hot, dry iron fuse the prepared appliqué shapes in place.

Step 4 Layer the prepared small heart and door on the prepared house shape and fuse in place.

Step 5 Buttonhole-stitch around the shapes using pearl cotton or 3 strands of embroidery floss. Also, buttonhole-stitch around the additional layered shapes.

Add the roof details to the house using the straight-stitch, as shown below.

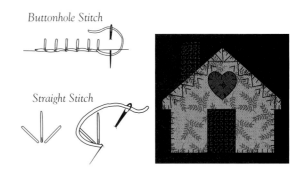

Note: To prevent the buttonhole-stitches from "rolling off" the edge of the appliqué shapes, take an extra backstitch in the same place as you make the buttonhole-stitch, going around outer curves, corners and points. For straight edges, taking a backstitch every inch is enough.

Step 6 With a hot, dry iron fuse the corresponding fusible web squares to the wrong side of the appliquéd BLACK PRINT squares. Referring to the heart diagram, trim the BLACK PRINT allowing 3/8-inch of the BLACK PRINT to extend beyond the applique edge. Peel off the paper backing.

Step 7 Position the prepared appliqué shapes on the 12-1/2 x 28-1/2-inch RED rectangle and fuse in place with a hot, dry iron.

Buttonhole-stitch the appliqué shapes in place.

Borders
Cutting
From BLACK PRINT:
- Cut 3, 2-1/2 x 42-inch inner border strips
- Cut 4, 4-1/2-inch corner squares

From RED PRINT:
- Cut 2, 4-1/2 x 42-inch strips for pieced border

From GREEN PRINT:
- Cut 2, 4-1/2 x 42-inch strips for pieced border

Attaching the Borders

Step 1 To attach the 2-1/2-inch wide BLACK inner borders, refer to page 138 for Border Instructions.

Step 2 Aligning long edges, sew together the 4-1/2 x 42-inch RED and GREEN strips in pairs, and press. Cut the strip sets into segments.

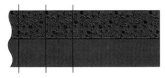

Crosscut 12, 4-1/2-inch wide segments

Step 3 Sew 2 segments together for the side pieced borders, and press. Sew the border strips to the runner, and press.

Step 4 Sew 4 segments together for the top and bottom pieced borders, and press. Add the 4-1/2-inch BLACK corner squares to both ends of the pieced border strips, and press. Sew the border strips to the runner, and press.

Putting It All Together

Trim the backing fabric and batting so they are 4-inches larger than the runner top. Refer to Finishing the Quilt on page 139 for complete instructions.

Binding

Cutting

From BLACK PRINT:
• Cut 4, 2-3/4 x 42-inch strips

Sew the binding to the quilt using a 3/8-inch seam allowance. This measurement will produce a 1/2-inch wide finished double binding. Refer to page 139 for Binding and Diagonal Piecing Instructions.

Holiday Table Topper

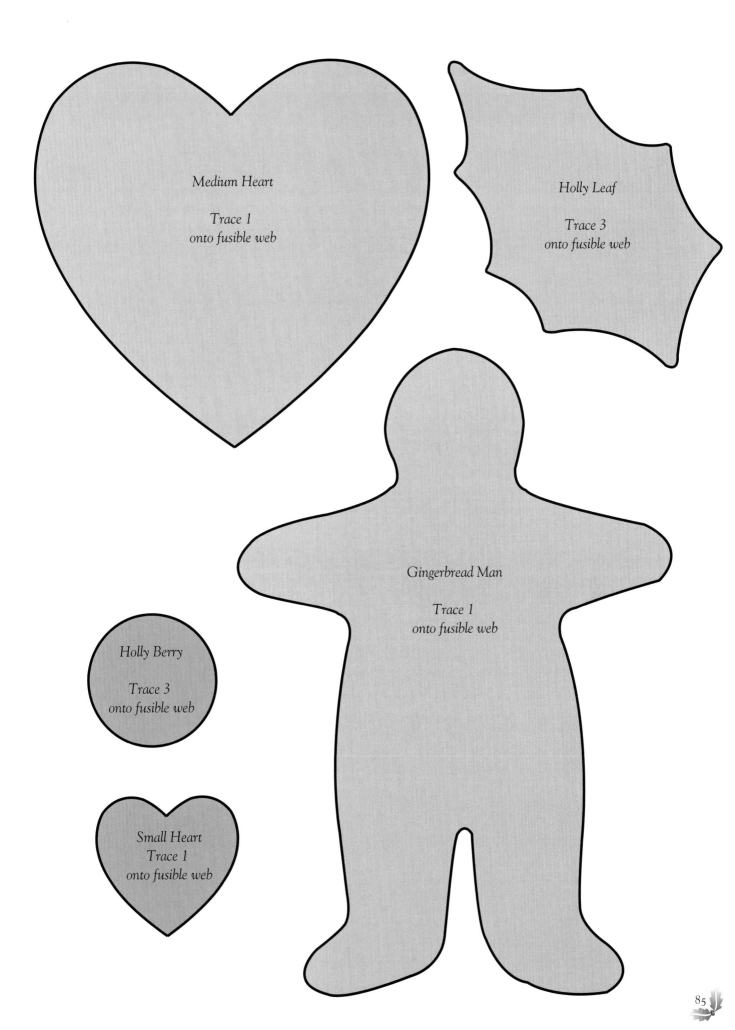

Medium Heart

Trace 1
onto fusible web

Holly Leaf

Trace 3
onto fusible web

Gingerbread Man

Trace 1
onto fusible web

Holly Berry

Trace 3
onto fusible web

Small Heart
Trace 1
onto fusible web

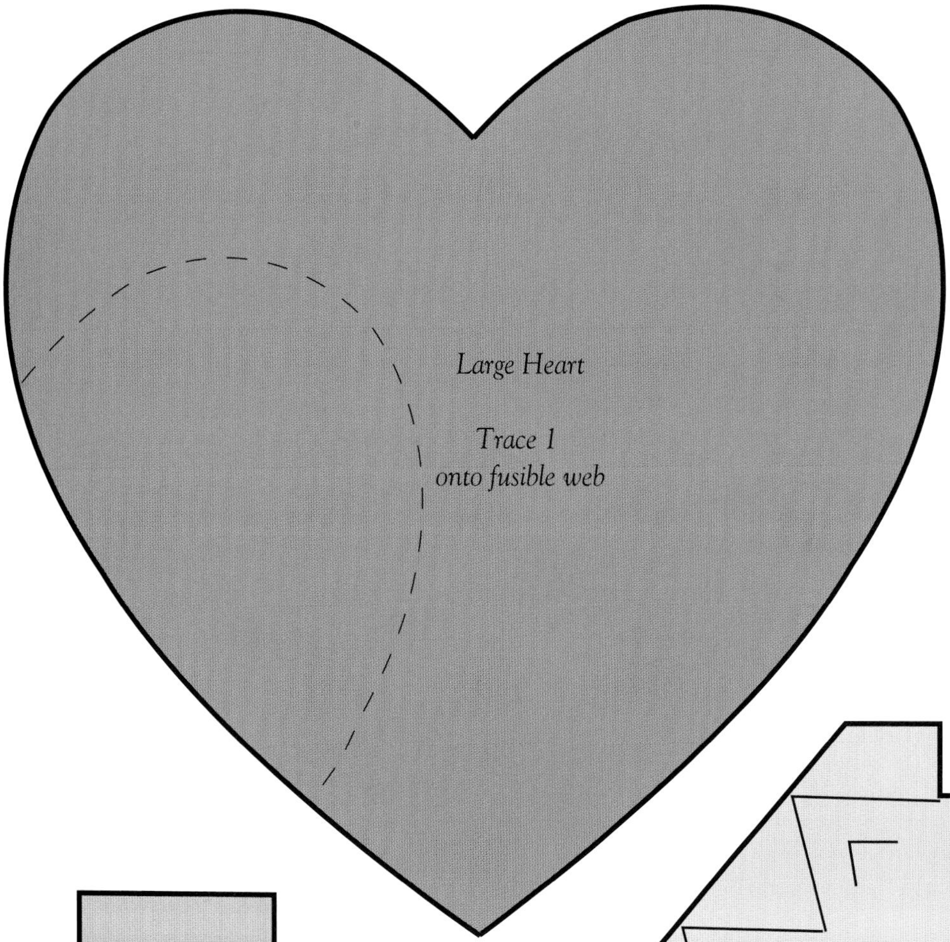

Large Heart

Trace 1
onto fusible web

Chimney

Trace 1
onto fusible web

Door

Trace 1
onto fusible web

House

Trace 1
onto fusible web

When the previous owners of the cottage moved, they took the rug covering the porch floor with them, leaving only the plywood underlayment. Rather than lay a new floor, Lynette cleverly designed quilt block stencils that she used for "painting" a quilt onto the sanded and sealed plywood floor. For the motifs she combined a winter snowflake and a wreath of spring, summer, and autumn leaves to create a four-season floor for the all-season porch.

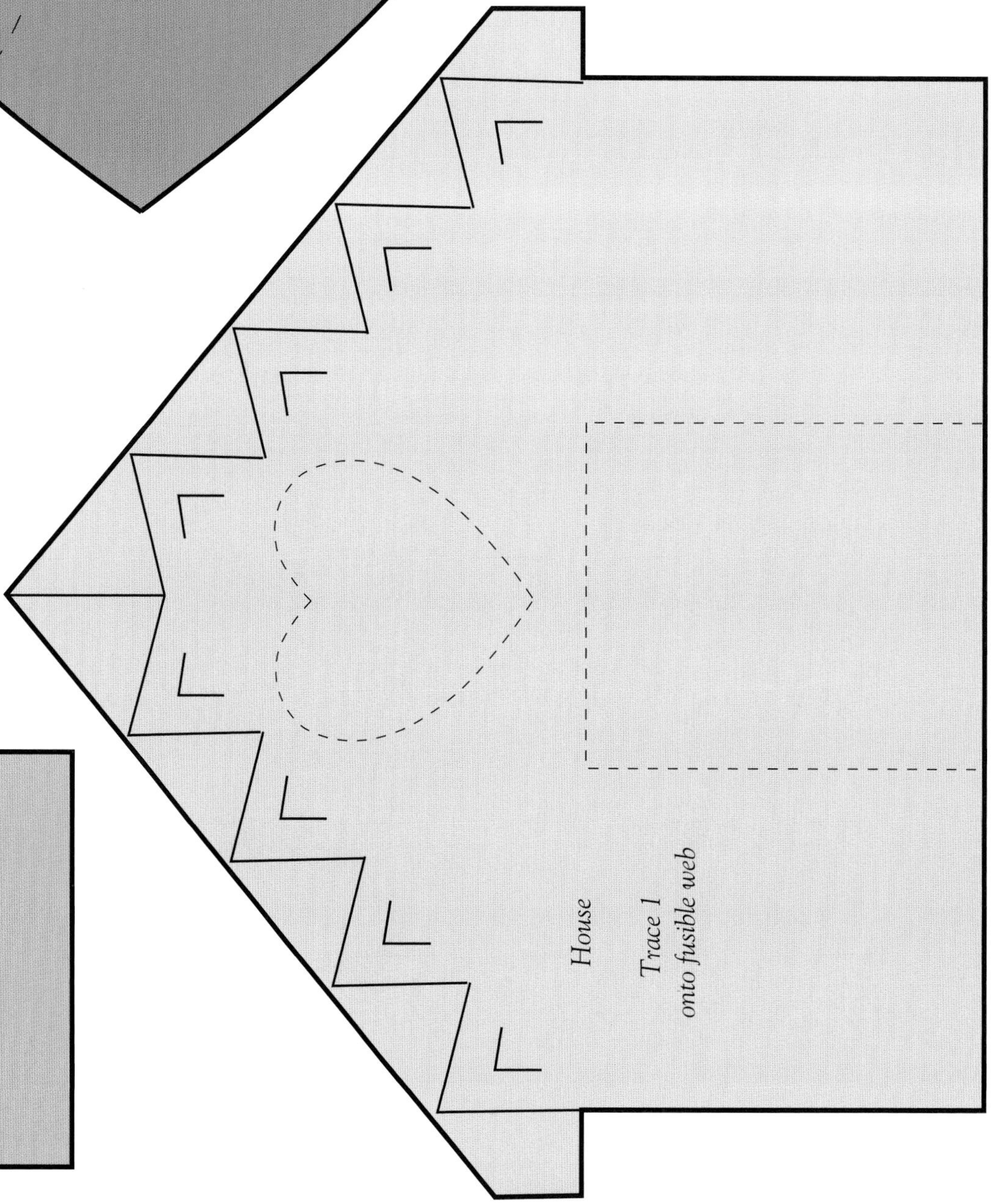

The Stenciled Floor Wreath is shown on page 87.

WHAT YOU'LL NEED

TEMPLATE PLASTIC

PERMANENT MARKING PEN

X-ACTO® KNIFE

Self-healing CUTTING MAT

STENCIL BRUSH AND PAINTS

General Stenciling

Step 1 Trace stencil onto template plastic with permanent marking pen.

Step 2 Lay the template plastic on the self-healing cutting mat. Using an X-Acto® knife cut out the stencil design.

Step 3 Using the dry brush technique (see below), stencil design onto floor, working from the outside of the design to the inside.

Dry Brush Technique

Step 1 Pour a small amount of paint onto a disposable coated plate.

Step 2 Dip tip of the dry stencil brush into paint.

Step 3 Wipe off excess paint on a paper towel until brush is "dry." Do this by pouncing the brush in an up and down motion to evenly distribute the paint and rid it of excess paint.

Step 4 Place stencil on the surface to be stenciled and hold the brush perpendicular to the stencil.

Step 5 Using a gentle circular motion, work around the edges of the stencil to the inside. Generally, stencils have lighter centers than edges, giving the design some highlights and interest. Reload the brush as necessary. Always remember to wipe off excess paint and continue to work with a "dry" brush.

Note: *There are stencil adhesive sprays available that help hold the edges of the stencil securely to the surface. Follow the manufacturer's instructions.*

Floor Layout

Note: *Floor squares are 17-inches square. The diagonal measurement of the square is 24-inches. These two measurements are needed to determine the layout of central design.*

Step 1 Prime and paint floor desired neutral base color. (I used Benjamin Moore #959.)

Step 2 Determine how central floor design will work for your floor.

Step 3 Lightly pencil in lines of blocks and borders. It will take considerable time to measure and plan, but it is a very important step.

Step 4 Use blue painter's tape to mask off blocks that will be sponged with a lighter color paint (off white). These blocks will be stenciled with wreath motif. Use a dry sponge. Place a small amount of paint in a flat pan. Dip sponge into paint and dab off excess. With a light, up and down motion, sponge the squares you have taped off. Let dry 1 hour.

Step 5 Trace snowflake stencil onto template plastic. With X-Acto® knife, cut out the stencil design.

Step 6 Using the dry brush stenciling technique, stencil snowflakes on alternating squares. Let dry 1 hour.

Step 7 Trace remaining stencils for wreath, leaves, and berries onto template plastic. Cut stencils.

Step 8 Stencil wreath base first. Let dry 1 hour. Position leaf stencils over previously stenciled wreath. Use a clean, dry brush when changing colors. Place leaves randomly using picture as a guide. Stencil all the same colored leaves at one time. Then stencil the second colored leaves. Add berries. Always use a clean dry brush when changing colors.

Step 9 Tape off the narrow border. This width can vary depending on your floor size. Use a 2-inch-wide and a 1-inch-wide wide foam brush to paint the checkerboard design on your floor.

Step 10 Outer border width will vary depending on your floor size. It should be at least 2-inches wider than the leaf stencil. Trace the stem and vine stencil separately from the leaves. Stencil vine first. Let dry 1 hour. Stencil leaves.

Step 11 Let finished floor dry at least 24 hours. Seal floor with 2 coats of polyurethane.

17-inch square

24-inch diagonal

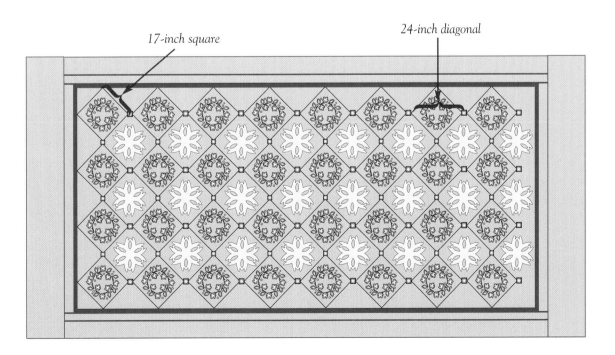

NOTE: When cutting stencils, allow an extra 2 inches of stencil template plastic beyond the cut stencil design.

Floor Border Stencil
&
Christmas Hideaway Wall Stencil

Trace and cut the vine stencil from template plastic.

Trace and cut the leaf stencil from template plastic.

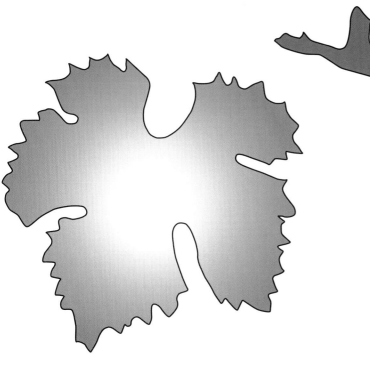

Wreath Base

Trace onto 17-inch paper square,
to get the complete wreath design,
then trace onto template plastic.

One-half of Floor Wreath Stencil

Floor Stencil Leaves

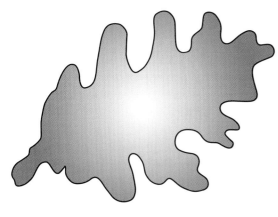

Floor Stencil Cherries

Red Square Stencil
at Block Intersection

Green Square Stencil
at Block Intersection

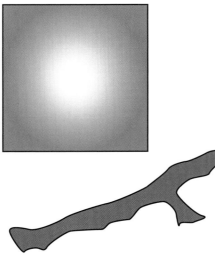

91

Floor Snowflake Stencil
This stencil must be enlarged to 210%

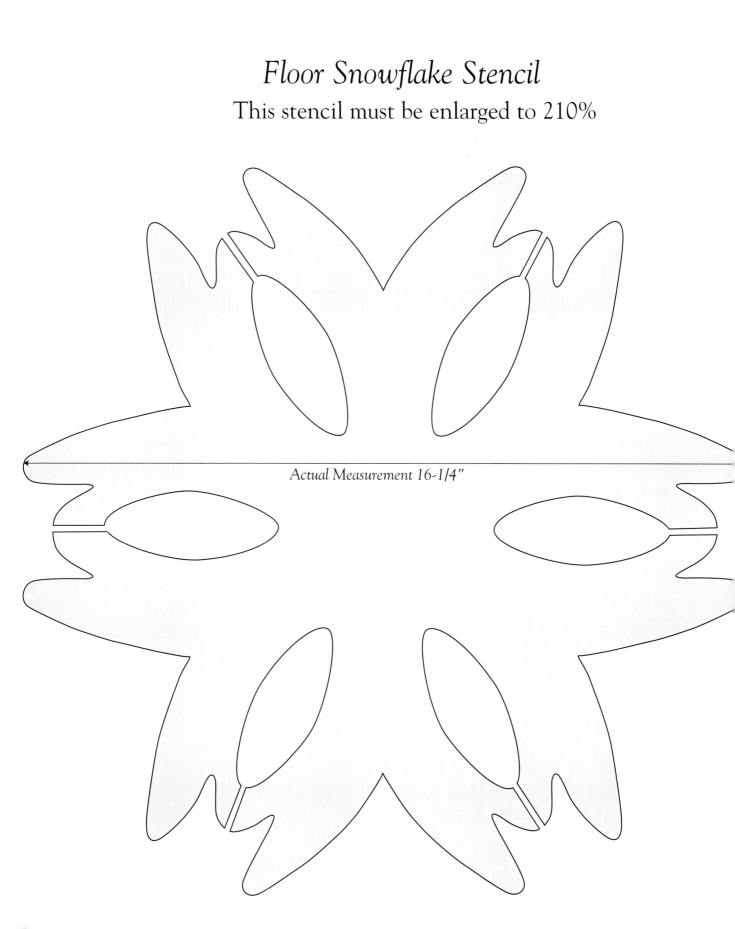

Actual Measurement 16-1/4"

Floor Wreath Stencil

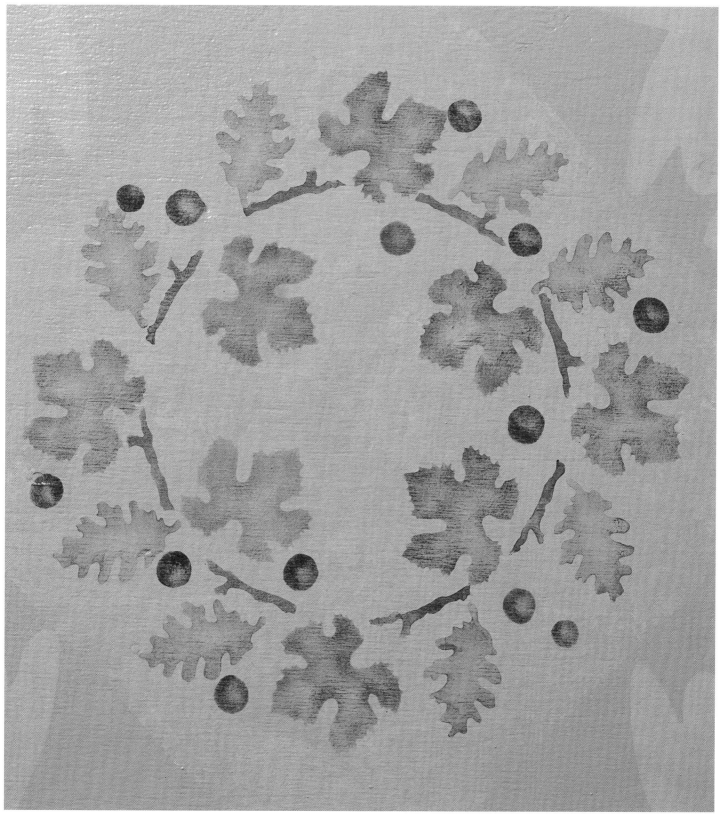

CHRISTMAS
stars & stripes

For a star-spangled salute to Christmas, celebrate with stenciled stars and ticking stripes in a spirited holiday mix of red, white, and blue.

For a room brimming with red, white, and blue holiday spirit, Lynette begins with a collection of red and blue quilts and ticking accessories. In the large photograph on the opposite page, the bedspread is made entirely of 6-1/2-inch squares of a variety of floral decorating fabrics and ticking stripes. The pillows are made from antique ticking and new decorator fabric. On the window seat in the background, greens are arranged in stacked oval tubs. The tubs are old—possibly two different sizes of bathtubs. For color and texture, wool snowflakes are stitched onto a blue wool blanket backed with flannel for the warmest blanket ever!

A TRIBUTE TO OLD GLORY. Flags fly and Santa smiles at Christmastime in this red, white, and blue bedroom. The framed flags are needlework and the antique pressed paper Santa is of German origin.

SOFTER VERSIONS OF RED, WHITE, AND BLUE. Lynette adds soft touches of color to the corner with a wooden rack filled with antique quilts and framed pieces—a miniature blue churn dash quilt and redwork embroidery—for the wall.

For Lynette, a room is not complete until the finished touches have been added. She makes sure that every nook and cranny gets special treatment for the holidays.

SPECIAL TREATS FOR GUESTS. The guest room gift tray holds towels, bedding, individual peppermint soaps, and a box of chocolates to welcome guests and make them feel extra special.

ALWAYS ROOM FOR MORE. The shelf above the blue iron bed is laden with greens, wrapped packages, and paper maché boots popular during the 1930's. Lynette designed new stars and stripes stockings and interspersed them with vintage hand knit stockings for a wall-full of old-fashioned fun.

The Stars & Stripes Stencil is shown throughout the bedroom and measures about 4-inches in width.

WHAT YOU'LL NEED

TEMPLATE PLASTIC

X-ACTO® KNIFE

Self-healing CUTTING MAT

STENCIL BRUSH

Stars & Stripes Stenciling

Step 1 Trace stencil onto stencil plastic.

Step 2 Lay the template plastic on the self-healing cutting mat. Using an X-Acto® knife, cut out the stencil design.

Step 3 With the dry brush technique (see below) stencil design onto walls, working from the outside of the design to the inside.

Step 4 Alternate stripes with stars.

Dry Brush Technique

Step 1 Pour a small amount of paint onto a disposable coated plate.

Step 2 Dip tip of the dry stencil brush into paint.

Step 3 Wipe off excess paint on a paper towel until brush is "dry." Do this by pouncing the brush in an up and down motion to evenly distribute the paint and rid it of excess paint.

Step 4 Place stencil on the surface to be stenciled and hold the brush perpendicular to the stencil.

Step 5 Using a gentle circular motion, work around the edges of the stencil to the inside. Generally, stencils have lighter centers than edges, giving the design some highlights and interest. Reload the brush as necessary. Always remember to wipe off excess paint and continue to work with a "dry" brush.

There are stencil adhesive sprays available that help hold the edges of the stencil securely to the surface. Follow manufacturer's instructions.

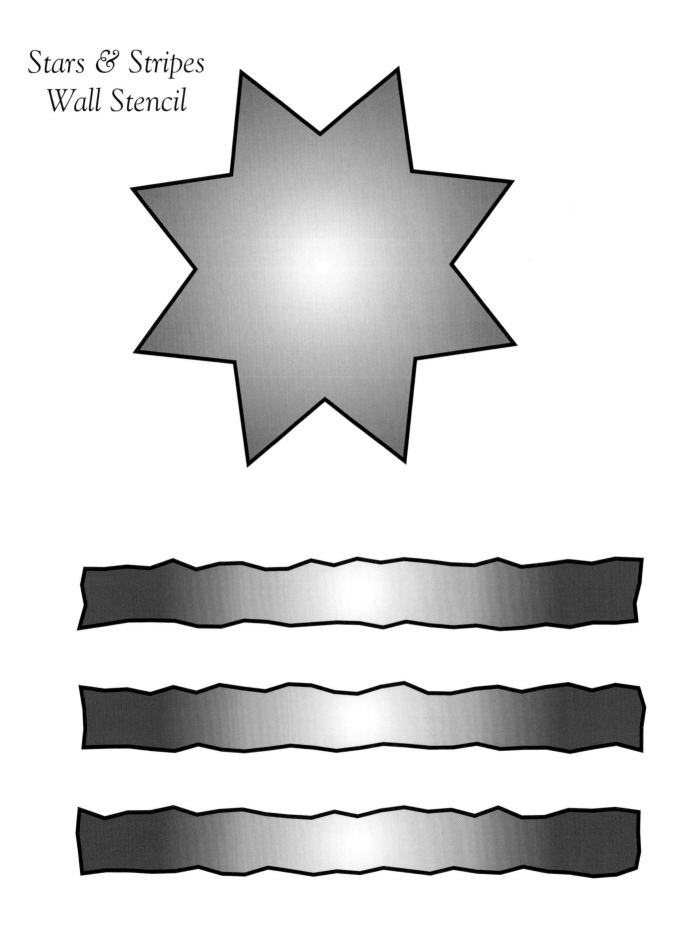

Stars & Stripes
Wall Stencil

Chevron Stocking

The Chevron Stocking shown
on page 95 measures 17-1/2-inches long.

What you'll need

Yardage is based on 42-inch wide fabric

1/8 yard GOLD PRINT
for chevron blocks

1/8 yard BEIGE PRINT
for chevron blocks

5/8 yard BLUE PRINT for stocking
front, stocking back and binding

6 x 12-inch piece
TICKING STRIPE for cuff

1/2 yard MUSLIN for lining

PELLON® FLEECE,
at least 14 x 42-inches

8-inch length of
RICKRACK for hanger

Stocking Front Assembly

Cutting

From GOLD PRINT:
- Cut 1, 2 x 42-inch strip.
  From this strip, cut:
  3, 2 x 3-1/2-inch rectangles
  6, 2-inch squares

From BEIGE PRINT:
- Cut 1, 2 x 42-inch strip.
  From this strip cut:
  3, 2 x 3-1/2-inch rectangles
  6, 2-inch squares

From BLUE PRINT:
- Cut 1, 14 x 20-inch rectangle
  for stocking back (set aside)
- Cut 2, 5 x 18-1/2-inch rectangles
- Cut 1, 3-1/2 x 4-1/2-inch rectangle
- Cut 1, 3-1/2-inch square
- Cut 1, 2-3/4 x 16-inch binding strip
  (set aside)
- Cut 2, 1-1/2 x 3-1/2-inch rectangles

From TICKING STRIPE:
- Cut 2, 5-inch squares.
  Cut the squares in half diagonally
  to make 4 triangles.

Piecing

Step 1 Position a 2-inch BEIGE square on the
corner of a 2 x 3-1/2 inch GOLD
rectangle. Draw a diagonal line on the
BEIGE square and stitch on the line.
Trim the seam allowance to 1/4-inch and
press. Repeat this process at the opposite
corner of the GOLD rectangle.

 *Make 3*

Step 2 Position a 2-inch GOLD square on the corner of a 2 x 3-1/2-inch BEIGE rectangle. Draw a diagonal line on the GOLD square and stitch on the line. Trim the seam allowance to 1/4-inch and press. Repeat this process at the opposite corner of the BEIGE rectangle. Sew a Step 1 unit to the top of each of these units and press. At this point each chevron block should measure 3-1/2 inches square.

Make 3   *Make 3*

Step 3 Referring to the diagram, sew together the 3 chevron blocks and the 1-1/2 x 3-1/2-inch BLUE rectangles. Sew the 3-1/2-inch BLUE square to the top edge of the unit and sew the 3-1/2 x 4-1/2-inch BLUE rectangle to the bottom edge and press. Add a 5 x 18-1/2-inch BLUE rectangle to both sides of the chevron unit and press.

Step 4 Refer to Basic Stocking Assembly Instructions on page 65 to assemble the stocking front and back.

Step 5 To make the TICKING STRIPE cuff units, with right sides together, sew the triangles together in pairs. Sew on one of the straight of grain edges and on the bias edge, referring to the diagram. Turn the units right side out and press. Baste the raw edges together.

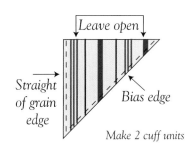

Leave open

Straight of grain edge   *Bias edge*

Make 2 cuff units

Step 6 Aligning raw edges, position the cuff units on the outside and at the top edge of the stocking. The cuff units should overlap at the center

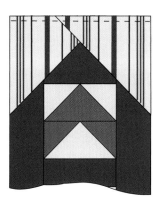

and the side edge of each cuff unit should be aligned with a stocking side seam. Baste in place. Refer to Basic Stocking Assembly Instructions on page 65 to add the binding and the rick-rack hanger to the stocking.

Stars & Stripes Stocking

The Stars & Stripes Stocking is shown on page 95 and measures 17-1/2-inches long.

WHAT YOU'LL NEED

Yardage is based on 42-inch wide fabric

5/8 yard STRIPE fabric for stocking front, stocking back, and cuff

3-1/2 x 42-inch strip TICKING STRIPE for hanger and binding

1/2 yard MUSLIN for lining

PELLON® FLEECE, at least 14 x 42-inches

Stocking Assembly

Cutting

From STRIPE:
- Cut 2, 14 x 20-inch rectangles (one for the stocking front and one for the stocking back)
- Cut 1, 7 x 13-inch strip for cuff

Assembly

Step 1 Refer to Basic Stocking Assembly Instructions on page 65 to assemble the stocking front and back.

Step 2 To make the cuff unit, with right sides together, sew the short ends of the 7 x 13-inch rectangle together and press. Fold the unit in half lengthwise with wrong sides together and right side facing out. Baste the raw edges together.

Step 3 Aligning raw edges, position the cuff unit on the outside and at the top edge of the stocking.

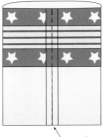

Seam line

Baste in place. Refer to Basic Stocking Assembly Instructions on page 65 to add the binding and the hanger to the stocking.

Baste

Baste

The Ticking Pillow is shown on page 97 and measures 16-inches square.

What you'll need

Yardage is based on 42-inch wide fabric

1-1/8 yards STRIPE for pillow front, back, and patches

3/8 yard Paper-backed fusible web

16-inch pillow form

#8 black pearl cotton, embroidery floss, or machine embroidery/topstitching thread for decorative stitches

Cutting

From Stripe fabric:
- Cut 2, 17 x 21-inch rectangles for pillow back
- Cut 1, 17-inch square for pillow front
- Cut 1, 4-1/2 x 18-inch rectangle for patches

From Fusible Web:
- Cut 1, 4-1/2 x 18-inch strip

Assembly

Step 1 Following the manufacturer's instructions, apply the fusible web strip to the wrong side of the 4-1/2 x 18-inch Stripe rectangle. Let the fabric cool and cut 4, 4-1/2-inch squares. Peel away the paper backing from the fusible web.

Step 2 Position the prepared patches on the 17-inch Stripe square. With a hot, dry iron fuse the patches in place.

Step 3 Buttonhole-stitch around the patches using pearl cotton or 3 strands of embroidery floss. If your machine has a buttonhole-stitch setting, use machine-embroidery/topstitching thread to add the decorative stitches.

Step 4 With wrong sides together, fold the 2, 17 x 21-inch Stripe rectangles in half to form 2, 10-1/2 x 17-inch double-thick pillow back pieces. Overlap the 2 folded edges by about 6-inches so the pillow back measures 17-inches square, and pin. Stitch around the entire piece to create a single pillow back.

Step 5 With right sides together, layer the pillow back and the pillow front, and pin. Stitch around the out-side edges using a 1/2-inch seam allowance.

Overlap

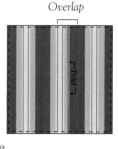

Step 6 Trim the pillow back and corner seam allowances if needed. Turn the pillow right side out. Insert the pillow form through the back opening.

CHRISTMAS *for friends*

Lynette treats friends and family to a hearty helping of hospitality with sweet treats from her kitchen served up in a dining room brimming with holiday bounty.

Star Sugar Cookies

> 3 CUPS FLOUR
> 1/2 TSP. SODA
> 1/2 TSP. BAKING POWDER
> I TSP. SALT
> I CUP BUTTER

Cut butter into dry ingredients with a pastry blender or with a fork as if making pie crust.

> I CUP SUGAR
> 2 EGGS
> I TSP. VANILLA

Mix together and then add to flour mixture. Roll out (thin) and cut with cookie cutters. Bake at 350 degrees for about 8 to 10 minutes. Edges should be slightly golden.

Makes about 48.

Ginger Sparkle Cookies

> I CUP SHORTENING
> I CUP GRANULATED SUGAR
> I CUP LIGHT MOLASSES
> I T. VINEGAR
> 2 SLIGHTLY BEATEN EGGS
> 5-1/2 CUPS FLOUR
> I TSP. CINNAMON
> I TSP. GINGER
> I TSP. SODA
> 1/2 TSP. SALT

Combine shortening, sugar, molasses and vinegar in a 2-quart saucepan. Bring slowly to a boil. Remove from heat and cool to room temperature. Add eggs to cooled mixture.

Mix flour, cinnamon, ginger, soda, and salt together and stir into the molasses mixture until dough is smooth and satiny. (At this point, dough is extremely soft, but it firms up when it is refrigerated.)

Divide into two portions. Wrap in plastic wrap and chill for at least 1 hour. Roll out dough to 1/4-inch thickness and cut with a fluted round cutter. Bake on lightly greased tins at 375 degrees for 8 minutes.

Makes about 4 dozen (amount depends on cookie cutter size).

Cookie Brittle

MIX TOGETHER:

1 CUP BUTTER

1-1/2 TSP. VANILLA

1 TSP. SALT

MIX TOGETHER AND GRADUALLY ADD:

1 CUP SUGAR

2 CUPS FLOUR

ADD:

1, 6 OZ. PKG. CHOCOLATE CHIPS

Press into non-greased 15 x 10-inch baking pan and sprinkle 1/2 cup chopped nuts over the top.

Bake at 375 degrees for 20 to 25 minutes. Cool and break apart.

Scandinavian Almond Bars

MIX TOGETHER AND SET ASIDE:

1-3/4 CUPS FLOUR

2 TSP. BAKING POWDER

1/4 TSP. SALT

IN A LARGE MIXING BOWL BEAT
    UNTIL SOFTENED:

1/2 CUP BUTTER OR MARGARINE

ADD:

1 CUP SUGAR AND BEAT UNTIL FLUFFY

ADD TO BUTTER/SUGAR MIXTURE AND
THEN BEAT ALL TOGETHER:

1 EGG

1/2 TSP. ALMOND EXTRACT

ALMOND ICING:

1 CUP SIFTED POWDERED SUGAR

1/4 TSP ALMOND EXTRACT

3 - 4 TSP. MILK

Divide dough into four equal parts and form each one into a 12-inch roll. Place two of the rolls 4 to 5 inches apart on a non-greased cookie sheet and flatten dough so it is about 3 inches wide. Repeat with last two rolls.

Brush with milk. Sprinkle with sliced almonds.

Bake at 325 degrees for 12 to 14 minutes. Edges should be slightly browned. Cut into 1-inch diagonal strips while bars are still warm. Cool and then drizzle with almond icing. Makes about 48.

Stir together powdered sugar and almond extract. Add milk to make thin consistency and drizzle over bars.

In the cottage dining room, shelves and cupboards filled to overflowing are the perfect backdrop for a treat-filled holiday table.

SERVE UP SOME SURPRISES. Lynette uses her green and cream flower pot collection to create an unexpected grouping with vintage tree and reindeer candles. She tucks candy canes and ribbon candy into the pots to add holiday color throughout.

DISPLAY YOUR FAVORITE PIECES. Lynette fills the hutch with brown and cream dishes, collectible glassware, and vintage tin baskets complemented by a late 1800's quilt hung on the door. A tray on the cupboard top is the backdrop for greens, pine cones, and hydrangeas.

Christmas for friends

Lynette transforms the side table in the dining room into a wonderland of natural abundance topped by a magnificent harvest wreath. For a romantic cottage glow, candles of various heights are placed on a platter and surrounded by greens, apples, and clove-studded orange pomanders for fragrance.

FILL THE ROOM WITH SONG. The songbird pictures are Lynette's flea market finds dressed up for the holidays with mats made from pages of an old music book. The sheets of music were folded as prairie points (a quilt edging technique) to surround the mat at the outer edges.

OLD-FASHIONED AMBIENCE. Tucked in a corner beside the dining room window, a small chest holds vintage tin floral baskets and holiday accents. The vintage artwork and spoon rack shelf holding greens and a candle complete the nostalgic mood.

CHRISTMAS Hideaway

Take a sabbatical from stress—on a daily basis! Whether it's breakfast in bed, an afternoon nap, or snuggling up in a quilt for a blissful evening with a good book, this room is for you! The deep hues of Christmas green and red with accents of cream and charcoal, transform any bedroom into a restful retreat.

The Cottage Throw is shown
on page 117 and measures 72 x 84-inches.

WHAT YOU'LL NEED

Yardage is based on 42-inch wide fabric

2 yards DARK GREEN PRINT for
pieced blocks

2 yards RED PRINT for pieced
blocks and corner squares

3-1/2 yards BEIGE PRINT
for background

2-1/2 yards GREEN FLORAL
for inner and outer borders

3/4 yard RED PRINT for binding

5 yards Backing fabric

Quilt batting,
at least 76 x 88-inches

Pieced Blocks (Make 24)

Cutting

From DARK GREEN PRINT:
- Cut 16, 3-1/2 x 42-inch strips.
  From these strips cut:
  96, 3-1/2 x 6-1/2-inch rectangles

From RED PRINT:
- Cut 16, 3-1/2 x 42-inch strips.
  From these strips cut:
  96, 3-1/2 x 6-1/2-inch rectangles

From BEIGE PRINT:
- Cut 35, 3-1/2 x 42-inch strips.
  From these strips cut:
  384, 3-1/2-inch squares

Piecing

Step 1 Position a 3-1/2-inch BEIGE square on
the corner of a 3-1/2 x 6-1/2-inch
RED rectangle. Draw a diagonal line
on the BEIGE square, and stitch on the

line. Trim the seam
allowance to 1/4-inch, and
press. Repeat this process at
the opposite corner of the
RED rectangle.

Unit A
Make 96

Step 2 Position a 3-1/2-inch BEIGE
square on the corner of a
3-1/2 x 6-1/2-inch DARK
GREEN rectangle. Draw a
diagonal line on the BEIGE
square, and stitch on the line. Trim the
seam allowance to 1/4-inch, and press.
Repeat this process at the opposite corner
of the GREEN rectangle, referring to the
diagram for stitching direction.

Unit B
Make 96

Step 3 Sew the A and B units
together in pairs to make
the C units, and press.
Sew the C units together
in pairs to make the D
units, and press.

Unit B
Unit A

Unit C
Make 96

Unit D
Make 48

Step 4 Assemble the block by sewing the D units together in pairs, and press. At this point each block should measure 12-1/2-inches square.

Make 24

Quilt Center

Cutting

From GREEN FLORAL:
- Cut 4, 6-1/2 x 42-inch inner border strips

Assembly

Step 1 Referring to the quilt diagram, sew the blocks together in 3 horizontal rows of 2 blocks each. Press the seam allowances in alternating directions by rows so the seams will fit snugly together with less bulk.

Step 2 Pin the rows at the block intersections and sew the rows together. Press the seam allowances in one direction. At this point the quilt center should measure 24-1/2 x 36-1/2-inches.

Step 3 To attach the 6-1/2-inch wide GREEN FLORAL inner border strips, refer to page 138 for Border Instructions.

Step 4 Sew together 3 blocks for the top edge and bottom edge of the quilt center, and press. Sew the strips to the quilt center, and press.

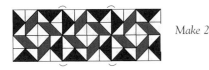
Make 2

Step 5 Sew together 6 blocks for each side of the quilt, and press. Sew the strips to the quilt center, and press.

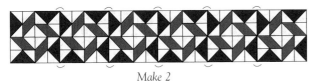
Make 2

Outer Border

Note: The yardage given allows for the border strips to be cut on the crosswise grain. Diagonally piece the strips as needed, referring to page 139 for Diagonal Piecing Instructions.

Cutting

From GREEN FLORAL:
- Cut 8, 6-1/2 x 42-inch outer border strips

From RED PRINT:
- Cut 4, 6-1/2-inch corner squares

Attaching the Border

Step 1 To attach the top and bottom 6-1/2-inch wide GREEN FLORAL outer border strips, refer to page 138 for Border Instructions.

Step 2 To attach the side 6-1/2-inch wide GREEN FLORAL outer border strips with 6-1/2-inch RED corner squares, refer to page 139 for Borders with Corner Squares.

Putting It All Together

Cut the 5-yard length of backing in half crosswise to make 2, 2-1/2 yard lengths. Refer to Finishing the Quilt on page 139 for complete instructions.

Binding

Cutting

From RED PRINT:
- Cut 9, 2-3/4 x 42-inch strips

Sew the binding to the quilt using a 3/8-inch seam allowance. This measurement will produce a 1/2-inch wide finished double binding. Refer to page 139 for Binding and Diagonal Piecing Instructions.

Cottage Throw

Patchwork Pillow Sham

The Patchwork Pillow Sham is shown on page 117 and measures 20-1/2 x 29-1/2-inches without the ruffle.

WHAT YOU'LL NEED

Yardage is based on 42-inch wide fabric

1/4 yard GREEN PLAID for blocks

1/2 yard BEIGE PRINT
for background

3/8 yard RED PRINT
for blocks and sawtooth border

1/4 yard RED PLAID for border

1-1/2 yards RED-and-GREEN
CHECK for ruffle (cut on the bias)

1-1/4 yards GREEN PLAID
for pillow back

Queen Bed Pillow
(21 x 29-inches)

Patchwork Pillow Sham

(Make 6 Blocks)

Cutting

From GREEN PLAID:
- Cut 1, 2-7/8 x 42-inch strip
- Cut 1, 1-7/8 x 14-inch strip.
  From this strip cut:
  6, 1-7/8-inch squares

From BEIGE PRINT:
- Cut 1, 2-7/8 x 42-inch strip
- Cut 3, 1-7/8 x 42-inch strips.
  From these strips cut:
  60, 1-7/8-inch squares.
  Cut the squares in half diagonally
  forming 120 triangles.

From RED PRINT:
- Cut 2, 1-7/8 x 42-inch strips.
  From these strips cut:
  24, 1-7/8-inch squares

Piecing

Step 1 With right sides together, sew a BEIGE triangle to one side of a 1-7/8-inch GREEN PLAID square, and press. Sew a BEIGE triangle to the opposite side of the GREEN PLAID square, and press. In the same manner, sew BEIGE triangles to the 2 remaining sides of the square, and press. At this point each square unit should measure 2-1/2-inches square. Adjust your seam allowances if needed.

Make 6

Step 2 With right sides together, sew a BEIGE triangle to one side of a 1-7/8-inch RED PRINT square, and press. Sew a BEIGE triangle to the opposite side of the RED PRINT square, and press. In the same manner, sew BEIGE triangles to the 2 remaining sides of the square, and press. At this point each square unit should measure 2-1/2-inches square. Adjust your seam allowances if needed.

Make 24

Step 3 With right sides together, layer together the 2-7/8 x 42-inch BEIGE and GREEN PLAID strips. Press together, but do not sew. Cut the layered strips into squares.

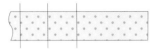

Crosscut 12, 2-7/8-inch squares

Make 24, 2-1/2-inch triangle-pieced squares

Cut the layered squares in half diagonally to make 24 sets of triangles. Stitch 1/4-inch from the diagonal edge of each set of triangles, and press. At this point each triangle-pieced square should measure 2-1/2-inches square.

Step 4 Referring to the block diagram, sew the units together in 3 horizontal rows. Press the seam allowances toward the BEIGE/RED square units. Sew the rows together and press. At this point each block should measure 6-1/2-inches square.

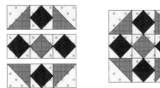

Make 6

Step 5 Referring to the Pillow Front diagram for placement, sew the blocks together in 2 horizontal rows of 3 blocks each, and press. At this point the pillow center should measure 12-1/2 x 18-1/2-inches.

Borders

Cutting

From RED PRINT:
- Cut 1, 3-7/8 x 42-inch strip for sawtooth border
- Cut 1, 3-1/2 x 42-inch strip. From this strip cut: 8, 3-1/2-inch squares

From BEIGE PRINT:
- Cut 1, 3-7/8 x 42-inch strip for sawtooth border
- Cut 1, 3-1/2 x 42-inch strip. From this strip cut: 4, 3-1/2 x 6-1/2-inch rectangles 4, 3-1/2-inch squares

From RED PLAID:
- Cut 1, 3-1/2 x 42-inch border strip
- Cut 2, 2 x 42-inch border strips

Piecing and Attaching the Borders

Step 1 With right sides together, layer together the 3-7/8 x 42-inch BEIGE and RED strips. Press together, but do not sew. Cut the layered strips into squares. Cut the layered squares in half diagonally to make 12 sets of triangles. Stitch 1/4-inch from the diagonal edge of each set of triangles, and press. At this point each triangle-pieced square should measure 3-1/2-inches square.

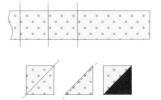

Crosscut 6, 3-7/8-inch squares

Make 12, 3-1/2-inch triangle-pieced squares

Step 2 Position a 3-1/2-inch RED square on the corner of a 3-1/2 x 6-1/2-inch BEIGE rectangle. Draw a diagonal line on the RED square, and stitch on the line. Trim the seam allowance to 1/4-inch, and press. Repeat this process at the opposite corner of the BEIGE rectangle. At this point each unit should measure 3-1/2 x 6-1/2-inches.

Make 4

Step 3 For the side sawtooth borders, sew Step 1 triangle-pieced squares to both sides of a Step 2 unit, and press. Make 2 border strips, sew them to the pillow center, and press.

Step 4 For the top and bottom borders, sew 2 of the Step 1 triangle-pieced squares to both sides of a Step 2 unit, and press. Add a 3-1/2-inch BEIGE square to both ends of the border strip, and press. Make 2 border strips, sew them to the pillow center, and press.

Step 5 To attach the side 3-1/2-inch wide RED PLAID border strips, refer to page 138 for Border Instructions.

Step 6 To attach the top and bottom 2-inch wide RED PLAID border strips, refer to page 138 for Border Instructions.

Ruffle

Cutting
From RED-and-GREEN CHECK:
- Cut enough 7-inch wide bias strips to make a 250-inch long strip

Attaching the Ruffle

Step 1 Piece the 7-inch wide RED-and-GREEN CHECK strips together to make a continuous ruffle strip.

Step 2 Fold the strip in half lengthwise,

wrong sides together, and press. Divide the ruffle strip into 4 equal segments, and mark the quarter points with safety pins.

Step 3 To gather the ruffle, position a heavy-weight thread (or 2 strands of regular weight sewing thread) 1/4-inch in from the raw edges of the folded ruffle strip.

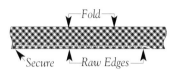

Fold

Secure — *Raw Edges*

Note: *You will need a length of heavyweight thread 184-inches long. Secure one end of the thread by stitching across it. Zigzag-stitch over the thread all the way around the ruffle, taking care not to sew through it.*

Step 4 Divide the edges of the pillow front into 4 equal segments and mark the quarter points with safety pins. With right sides together, pin the ruffle to the pillow front, matching the quarter points of the ruffle to the quarter points of the pillow front. Pull up the gathering stitches until the ruffle fits the pillow front, taking care to allow extra fullness in the ruffle at each corner. Sew the ruffle to the pillow front, using a 1/4-inch seam allowance.

Pillow Back

Cutting
From GREEN PLAID:
- Cut 2, 21 x 36-inch rectangles

Assembling the Pillow Back

Step 1 With wrong sides together, fold the 2, 21 x 36-inch GREEN PLAID rectangles in half to form 2, 18 x 21-inch double-thick pillow back pieces. Overlap the 2 folded edges by about 5-inches so the pillow back measures

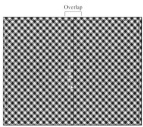

Overlap

21 x 30-inches, and pin. Stitch around the entire piece to create a single pillow back, using a scant 1/4-inch seam allowance.

Step 2   With right sides together, layer the pillow back and the pillow front, and pin. The ruffle will be turned toward the center of the pillow at this time. Stitch around the outside edges using a 1/2-inch seam allowance.

Step 3   Trim the pillow back and corner seam allowances if needed. Turn the pillow right side out and fluff up the ruffle. Insert the pillow form through the back opening.

Patchwork Pillow Front

Personalize a cottage bedroom with a few of your favorite things for a retreat that holds special meaning for you. If wall space is limited, Lynette uses a seldom-opened chest of drawers as a way to display a quilt in colors of the season for special occasions such as Christmas. The walls are painted sage green with slightly darker sage green ragged on to give texture. The room's border stencil (see page 90) uses the same green as the ragged texture to tie it all together.

STACK UP SOME HOLIDAY SPIRIT. A trio of mismatched shelves all painted the same color and hung as a unit create an unusual wall grouping.

EVEN THE BATH CAN BE HOLIDAY BRIGHT. The bathroom adjoining the bedroom retreat can be easy on the eyes with a few holiday touches. Lynette dressed up a small, wall-hung sink with a plaid gathered skirt secured with self-adhesive Velcro® tape. She used an old top-hat rack for towels in deep greens and red plaids.

COZY UP A CORNER. In the large photograph, opposite, a vintage sled holding a quilt is grouped with a Windsor rocker and table top tree packed full of fruit, autumn leaves, and dried hydrangea blossoms from Lynette's garden for a corner-full of comfort.

The Baby Bloom Quilt is shown on page 126 and measures 42 x 49-inches.

WHAT YOU'LL NEED

Yardage is based on 42-inch wide fabric

1/8 yard each of 5 ASSORTED RED PRINTS for flowers

2 yards BEIGE PRINT for background, lattice strips, nine-patch lattice posts, and outer border

1/3 yard GREEN PRINT for leaves

2/3 yard GOLD PRINT for lattice strips and nine-patch lattice posts

1/2 yard GOLD PRINT for binding

2-2/3 yards Backing fabric

Quilt Batting, at least 46 x 54-inches

Flower Blocks (Make 20)

Cutting

From *each* of the 5 ASSORTED RED PRINTS:
- Cut 4, 3-1/2-inch squares

From BEIGE PRINT:
- Cut 3, 2 x 42-inch strips.
  From these strips cut:
  60, 2-inch squares
- Cut 3, 1-1/4 x 42-inch strips.
  From these strips cut:
  80, 1-1/4-inch squares

From GREEN PRINT:
- Cut 4, 2 x 42-inch strips.
  From these strips cut:
  40, 2 x 3-1/2-inch rectangles

Piecing

Step 1   Position 1-1/4-inch BEIGE squares on the 4 corners of each of the 3-1/2-inch RED squares. Draw a diagonal line on each BEIGE square, and stitch on the line. Trim the seam allowance to 1/4-inch, and press.

Make 4 from each RED PRINT for a total of 20

Step 2   Position a 2-inch BEIGE square on the left-hand corner of a 2 x 3-1/2-inch GREEN rectangle. Draw a diagonal line on the BEIGE square, and stitch on the line. Trim the seam allowance to 1/4-inch, and press.

Make 20

Step 3 Repeat Step 2, this time reversing the direction of the seam line.

5Make 20

Step 4 Sew a Step 2 leaf unit to a Step 1 flower unit, and press.

Make 20

Step 5 Sew a Step 3 leaf unit to a 2-inch BEIGE square, and press.

Make 20

Step 6 Sew the Step 4 and Step 5 units together to complete the flower block. At this point each flower block should measure 5-inches square.

Make 20

Make 4 blocks from each RED PRINT for a total of 20 flower blocks

Nine-Patch Lattice Posts (Make 30)
Lattice Strips (Make 49)

Cutting

From GOLD PRINT:
• Cut 14, 1-1/2 x 42-inch strips

From BEIGE PRINT:
• Cut 19, 1-1/2 x 42-inch strips

Piecing

Note: The nine-patch lattice posts and lattice strips are made up of strip sets. Refer to page 138 for Hints and Helps for Pressing Strip Sets.

Step 1 Sew 1-1/2 x 42-inch BEIGE strips to both sides of a 1-1/2 x 42-inch GOLD strip. Press the seam allowances toward the GOLD strips. Make 8 strip sets. Cut the strip sets into 5-inch wide segments for lattice strips and 1-1/2-inch wide segments for nine-patch lattice posts.

Crosscut 49, 5-inch wide segments for lattice strips

Crosscut 30, 1-1/2-inch wide segments for nine-patch lattice posts

Step 2 Sew 1-1/2 x 42-inch GOLD strips to both sides of a 1-1/2 x 42-inch BEIGE strip. Press the seam allowances toward the GOLD strips. Make 3 strip sets. Cut the strip sets into segments.

Crosscut 60, 1-1/2-inch wide segments for nine-patch lattice posts

Step 3 Sew a Step 2 segment to both sides of a 1-1/2-inch wide Step 1 segment. At this point each nine-patch lattice post should measure 3-1/2-inches square.

Make 30

Quilt Center

Step 1 Referring to the quilt diagram for placement, sew together a horizontal row of 4 flower blocks alternating with 5 of the Step 1, 5-inch wide lattice strip segments, and press. Refer to the quilt diagram to determine which direction the flower blocks should face within each row. Make 5 block rows.

Step 2 To make the lattice strips, sew together a horizontal row of 5 nine-patch lattice posts and 4 of the Step 1, 5-inch wide lattice strip segments, and press. Make 6 lattice strips.

Step 3 Referring to the quilt diagram for placement, sew the block rows and lattice strips together, and press.

Border

Note: The yardage given allows for the border strips to be cut on the crosswise grain. Diagonally piece the strips as needed, referring to page 139 for Diagonal Piecing Instructions.

From BEIGE PRINT:
• Cut 5, 5 x 42-inch border strips

To attach the 5-inch wide BEIGE border strips, refer to page 138 for Border Instructions.

Putting It All Together

Cut the 2-2/3 yard length of backing fabric in half crosswise to make 2, 1-1/3 yard lengths. Refer to Finishing the Quilt on page 139 for complete instructions.

Binding

Cutting
From GOLD PRINT:
- Cut 5, 2-3/4 x 42-inch strips

Sew the binding to the quilt using a 3/8-inch seam allowance. This measurement will produce a 1/2-inch wide finished double binding. Refer to page 139 for Binding and Diagonal Piecing Instructions.

Baby Bloom Quilt

Cottage Pillow

*The Cottage Pillow is shown
on page 127 and measures 9 x 12-inches.*

WHAT YOU'LL NEED

Yardage is based on 42-inch wide fabric

**12 x 15-inch TAUPE
WOOL for pillow front**

**1/4 yard BLACK WOOL
for pillow back**

1/4 yard MUSLIN

**Polyester fiberfill for
inner pillow form**

**Black, taupe, and gray 6 ply
embroidery floss for decorative
stitch. Black and taupe
6 ply rayon for decorative stitches**

Iron-on transfer pencil

Pillow Front

Stitching

*The Cottage Pillow Design is on page 134
and the decorative stitches are on page 139.*

Step 1 Trace the outline of the Cottage
Pillow Design onto paper using the
iron-on transfer pencil, referring to
manufacturer's directions. Then, transfer
the design onto the TAUPE WOOL.

Step 2 Using the photo as a guide, outline
stitch the design in the corresponding
color, then fill in the design with long
and short satin stitches. Add the
French knots when the satin stitching
is complete.

House:

    Outline stitch in 2 ply black floss, fill in
the design with long and short satin
stitches using blended threads of 2 ply
black floss and 1ply black rayon floss.

Roof, tree, branches, and snow:

    Use long and short satin stitches in
blended threads of 2 ply taupe floss and
1 ply taupe rayon floss.

Door and window:

    Satin stitch in 2 ply gray floss. Use 2 ply
black floss to make a French knot for the
door knob.

Pine trees:

    Long and short satin stitches in blended
threads of 2 ply black floss and 1ply black
rayon floss.

Snowflakes:

Blended threads of 2 ply taupe and 1 ply rayon taupe in French knots.

Pillow Back

Cutting

From BLACK WOOL:
- Cut 2, 9 x 15-inch rectangles for pillow back

Assembling the Pillow Back

Step 1 Fold the 2 pillow back pieces in half, with wrong sides together, to form 2, 7-1/2 x 9-inch double-thick back pieces. Overlap the 2 folded edges by about 2-1/2-inches and stitch around the entire piece to create a single pillow back.

Step 2 Layer the pillow back and the completed pillow top, with right sides facing. Pin the edges of the pillow top and back together, and stitch around the outside edge, using a 1/4-inch seam allowance.

Step 3 Trim the pillow back and corner seam allowances if needed. Turn the pillow right side out. With matching thread, stitch 1/2-inch from the edge of the pillow to form an edge. With 3 strands of black embroidery floss, buttonhole-stitch the edge of the pillow using long/short stitches.

Inner Pillow Form

Cutting

From MUSLIN:
- Cut 2, 7-1/2 x 11-inch rectangles

Assembling the Pillow Form

Step 1 Sew together the 2, 7-1/2 x 11-inch muslin rectangles, using a 1/4-inch seam allowance. Leave a 5-inch long opening for turning.

Step 2 Turn the piece right side out and stuff firmly with polyester fiberfill. Hand-stitch the opening closed. Insert the pillow form through the back opening of the pillow case.

Cottage Pillow Design

The design is reversed for tracing purposes.
When the embroidery is finished it will appear as
in the photograph.

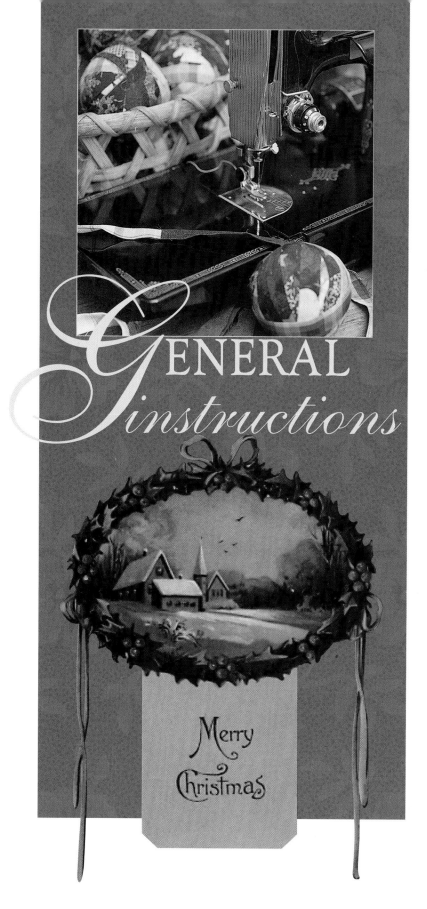

GENERAL Instructions

Merry Christmas

GETTING STARTED

- Yardage is based on 42"-wide fabric.

- A rotary cutter, mat, and wide clear plastic ruler with 1/8" markings are needed tools in attaining accuracy. A 6" x 24" ruler is recommended.

- Read instructions thoroughly before beginning project.

- Prewash and press fabrics.

- Place right sides of fabric pieces together and use 1/4" seam allowances throughout unless otherwise specified.

- Seam allowances are included in the cutting sizes given. It is very important that accurate 1/4" seam allowances are used. It is wise to stitch a sample 1/4" seam allowance to check your machine's seam allowance accuracy.

- Press seam allowances toward the darker fabric and/or in the direction that will create the least amount of bulk.

Hints and Helps from Lynette for: *Pressing Strip Sets*

When sewing strips of fabric together for strip sets, it is important to press the seam allowances nice and flat, usually to the darker fabric. Be careful not to stretch as you press, causing a "rainbow effect." This will affect the accuracy and shape of the pieces cut from the strip set. I like to press on the wrong side first and with the strips perpendicular to the ironing board. Then I flip the piece over and press on the right side to prevent little pleats from forming at the seams. Laying the strip set lengthwise on the ironing board seems to encourage the rainbow effect, as shown in diagram.

Avoid this rainbow effect

Borders

Note: Cut borders to the width called for. Always cut border strips a few inches longer than needed, just to be safe. Diagonally piece the border strips together as needed.

Step 1 With pins, mark the center points along all 4 sides of the quilt. For the top and bottom borders measure the quilt from left to right through the middle.

Step 2 Measure and mark the border lengths and center points on the strips cut for the borders before sewing them on.

Step 3 Pin the border strips to the quilt and stitch a 1/4" seam. Press the seam allowances toward the borders. Trim off excess border lengths.

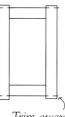

Trim away excess fabric

Step 4 For the side borders, measure your quilt from top to bottom, including the borders just added, to determine the length of the side borders.

Step 5 Measure and mark the side border lengths as you did for the top and bottom borders.

Step 6 Pin and stitch the side border strips in place. Press and trim the border strips even with the borders just added.

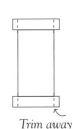

Trim away excess fabric

Step 7 If your quilt has multiple borders, measure, mark, and sew additional borders to the quilt in the same manner.

Borders with Corner Squares

Step 1 For the top and bottom borders, refer to Steps 1, 2, and 3 in **Borders**. Measure, mark, and sew the top and bottom borders to the quilt. Trim away excess fabric.

Step 2 For the side borders, measure just the quilt top including seam allowances, but not the top and bottom borders. Cut the side borders to this length. Sew a corner square to each end of these border strips. Sew the borders to the quilt, and press.

Decorative Stitches

Long & Short Buttonhole Stitch

Buttonhole Stitch

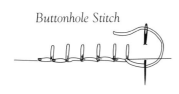

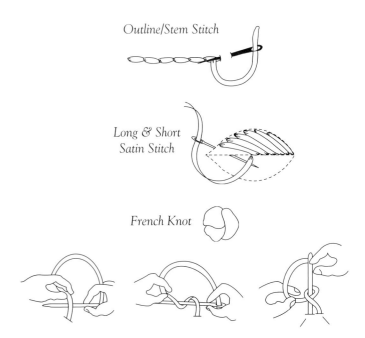

Outline/Stem Stitch

Long & Short Satin Stitch

French Knot

Finishing the Quilt

Step 1 Remove the selvages from the backing fabric. Sew the long edges together, and press. Trim the backing and batting so they are 2" to 4" larger than the quilt top.

Step 2 Mark the quilt top for quilting. Layer the backing, batting, and quilt top. Baste the 3 layers together and quilt.

Step 3 When quilting is complete, remove basting. Baste all 3 layers together a scant 1/4" from the edge. This hand-basting keeps the layers from shifting and prevents puckers from forming when adding the binding. Trim excess batting and backing fabric even with the edge of the quilt top. Add the binding as shown.

Binding and Diagonal Piecing

Diagonal Piecing

Stitch diagonally

Trim to 1/4" seam allowance

Press seam open

Step 1 Diagonally piece the binding strips. Fold the strip in half lengthwise, wrong sides together, and press.

Double-layer Binding

Step 2 Unfold and trim one end at a 45° angle. Turn under the edge 1/4" and press. Refold the strip.

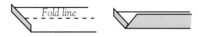

Fold line

Step 3 With raw edges of the binding and quilt top even, stitch with a 3/8" seam allowance, unless otherwise specified, starting 2" from the angled end.

Step 4 Miter the binding at the corners. As you approach a corner of the quilt, stop sewing 1/4 to 1/2" from the corner of the quilt. (Use the same measurement as your seam allowance).

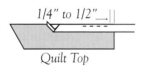

1/4" to 1/2"

Quilt Top

Step 5 Clip the threads and remove the quilt from under the presser foot.

Step 6 Flip the binding strip up and away from the quilt, then fold the binding down even with the raw edge of the quilt. Begin sewing at the upper edge. Miter all 4 corners in this manner.

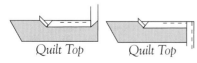

Quilt Top   *Quilt Top*

Step 7 Trim the end of the binding so it can be tucked inside of the beginning binding about 3/8". Finish stitching the seam.

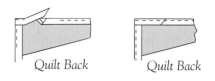

Quilt Back   *Quilt Back*

Step 8 Turn the folded edge of the binding over the raw edges and to the back of the quilt so that the stitching line does not show. Hand-sew the binding in place, folding in the mitered corners as you stitch.

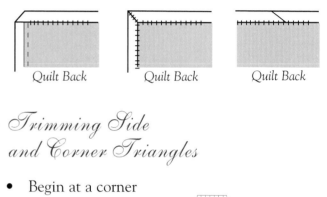

Quilt Back   *Quilt Back*   *Quilt Back*

Trimming Side and Corner Triangles

- Begin at a corner by lining up your ruler 1/4-inch beyond the points of the corners of the blocks as shown. Draw a light line along the edge of the ruler. Repeat this procedure on all four sides of the quilt top, lightly marking cutting lines.

  1/4"

  Mark cutting lines lightly 1/4" beyond the points of the corners of the blocks.

  1/4"   1/4"

  Make sure the corners are 90° angles before you cut.

- Check all the corners before you do any cutting. Adjust the cutting lines as needed to ensure square corners.

- When you are certain that everything is as square as it can be, position your ruler over the quilt top. Using your marked lines as guides, cut away the excess fabric with your rotary cutter, leaving a 1/4-inch seam allowance beyond the block corners.

Lynette Jensen's designs for the quilts and decorative accessories featured in
CHRISTMAS COTTAGE are available from her Thimbleberries®
line of books and patterns. Please call 800/587-3944 to order a catalog,
or for more information about obtaining patterns for the quilt shown below.

DECORATIVE SOURCES

Hurricane Candle Stand
(Star Spangled Sampler Co., 817/451-2627)

11

Reindeer Stag Tea Service (Austrian China)
(Frost and Budd, 952/ 473-1442)

22

Pewter Pitcher
(Star Spangled Sampler Co., 817/451-2627)

23

Artificial White Berry Garland
(Main Street Cotton Shop, 800/624-4001)

29

Waiting For Santa Quilt
(Thimbleberries®)

51

Crocheted Rug (*Classic Country*, by Lynette Jensen)
(A Landauer Publication, 800/557-2144)

51

Peppermint Soaps
(Crabtree and Evelyn)

98

Reindeer Towels
(Santens)

98

Holly Punch Set
(Personal Antique Collection)

107

Red/Green Quilt
(Personal Antique Quilt Collection)

107

PROJECT INDEX

Sheet Music Cone 18

Box Tree Ornament 20

Patchwork Pines Quilt 24

Homestead Quilt 30

Festive Bow Ties Wall Quilt 34

Country Village Ornaments 38

Leaf Stenciling 42

Brick Quilt 46

Napkins with Binding 47

Patchwork Blossom Pillow 48

Scottie Dog Quilt 52

Pinwheel/Rickrack Pillowcases 56

Kids Around the Block Quilt 58

Pinwheel Stocking 64

Snow Candle 75

Holiday Table Topper 82

Stenciled Floor Wreath 88

Stars & Stripes Stenciling 99

Chevron Stocking 101

Stars & Stripes Stocking 103

Ticking Pillow 104

Cottage Throw 118

Patchwork Pillow Sham 121

Baby Bloom Quilt 128

Cottage Pillow 132

THIMBLEBERRIES®